D0170316

BIKING OHIO'S
RAIL-TRAILS

Where to Go • What to Expect • How to Get There

by
Shawn E. Richardson

Adventure Publications

ADVENTURE PUBLICATIONS, INC.
P.O. Box 269
Cambridge, MN 55008
1-800-678-7006

Biking Ohio's Rail-Trails
Where to Go, What to Expect, How to Get There.

Revised 1997

ISBN 1-885061-16-1

Text, research, cartography, and photography by Shawn E. Richardson.
Additional editing by Dr. Harold E. Richardson.

Front cover:
Central photo: The Little Miami Scenic Trail near Yellow Springs, Ohio.

Back cover:
Top: The Towpath Trail follows the old Ohio-Erie Canal.
Middle: A scene along the Emerald Necklace Trail near Lakewood.
Bottom: The Towpath Trail traverses wetlands as a boardwalk.

Copyediting, interior design, and typesetting by
Tony Dierckins Publishing Services

This book is for Dr. Harold Edward and Antonia Calvert Richardson, Jill C. Richardson Lang, Tom Edwards and Mary Gleason Boone, Tom Edwards Boone Jr., Betsy Boone-Abraham, Steven M. Slucher, Tina Davy, Rob M. Longest, Michael Longest, Mark J. Ballenger, Yoon Kim, Bob G. Koenig, and Joyce A. Reoch for joining me in trailblazing across Ohio's rail-trails.

And to the Rails-to-Trails Conservancy and all the recreationalists who will blaze these trails.

Contents

INTRODUCTION

I researched and created Biking Ohio's Rail-Trails as a guide to Ohio's major off-road multipurpose trails and rail-trails. It provides tourists, weekend travelers, outdoor lovers, and recreationalists with a set of uniform, detailed maps that allow them to easily find each trail. The maps and text also help drivers find parking and other locations to drop off or pick up trail users. Maps of trails with permanent mile markers help users calculate the distance of their outdoor excursions.

Most of the trails described herein have a smooth surface to allow users to bicycle, mountain bicycle, walk, hike, roller skate, or travel by wheelchair. Many are open to cross country skiers during winter months and some even allow for horseback riding. Best of all, Ohio prohibits motorized vehicles from using the trails at any time, providing a safe alternative to users throughout the year. Check each individual trail to make sure it allows for your intended use.

While the book does not include maps for some shorter or limited-use trails, a description of each can be found under "Ohio's Minor Rail-Trails" on page 74. Addresses are provided so readers can obtain more information concerning these trails.

The maps and information in Biking Ohio's Rail-Trails are current as of 1997. Future editions will include trails currently under development, a list of which appears under "Ohio's Potential Rail-Trails" on page 76. If you find that any of the maps need corrections, or if you have discovered trails not listed, write to me at: Shawn E. Richardson, Biking USA's Rail-Trails, PO Box 284, Hilliard, OH 43026-0284. I hope this book makes trailblazing across the Buckeye State more convenient and enjoyable for you, and whenever you use these trails, always keep in mind the safety tips listed in the back of the book. Happy trails!

— Shawn E. Richardson, 1997

THE RAILS-TO-TRAILS CONSERVANCY

Founded in 1985 with the mission of enhancing America's communities and countrysides, the Rails-to-Trails Conservancy is a national nonprofit organization dedicated to converting abandoned rail corridors into a nationwide network of multipurpose trails. By linking parks, schools, neighborhoods, communities, towns, cities, states, and national parks, this system will connect important landmarks and create both a haven for wildlife and a safe place for able and handicapped adults and children to bicycle, walk, in-line skate, and travel by wheelchair. Rail-trails meet demands for local recreational opportunities and connect with long-distance trails to make it possible to ride continuously across a state and eventually even from coast to coast without encountering a motorized vehicle.

This vision of the Rails-to-Trails Conservancy is quickly becoming a reality. Over 700 trails totaling more than 7,000 miles have already been successfully converted into multipurpose trails in the United States, and another 1,000 rail-trails are in the works.

Since 1989 the Ohio Chapter of the Rail-to-Trails Conservancy has worked to establish the Discover Ohio Trails System, a statewide interconnected trail system utilizing abandoned rail corridors and canal towpaths. This 1,233-mile trail system will promote regional linkages and connect Ohio with all five of its bordering states. Grassroots efforts to save and convert rail-trails across Ohio have already resulted in 30 trails stretching 200 miles, and more than forty additional conversion projects are under way. Ohio leads the nation in rail-trails and one third of the ambitious Discover Ohio Trails System has already been funded for completion.

Your membership, support, and enthusiasm will help the Rail-to-Trails Conservancy and its Ohio Chapter continue to make their vision become a reality. See page 87 for information on how you can join the Rails-to-Trails Conservancy.

LEGEND

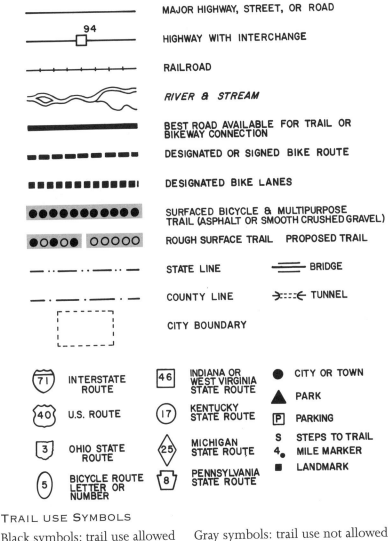

	MAJOR HIGHWAY, STREET, OR ROAD
94	HIGHWAY WITH INTERCHANGE
	RAILROAD
	RIVER & STREAM
	BEST ROAD AVAILABLE FOR TRAIL OR BIKEWAY CONNECTION
	DESIGNATED OR SIGNED BIKE ROUTE
	DESIGNATED BIKE LANES
	SURFACED BICYCLE & MULTIPURPOSE TRAIL (ASPHALT OR SMOOTH CRUSHED GRAVEL)
	ROUGH SURFACE TRAIL PROPOSED TRAIL
	STATE LINE BRIDGE
	COUNTY LINE TUNNEL
	CITY BOUNDARY

71	INTERSTATE ROUTE	46	INDIANA OR WEST VIRGINIA STATE ROUTE	●	CITY OR TOWN
40	U.S. ROUTE	17	KENTUCKY STATE ROUTE	▲	PARK
3	OHIO STATE ROUTE	25	MICHIGAN STATE ROUTE	P	PARKING
5	BICYCLE ROUTE LETTER OR NUMBER	8	PENNSYLVANIA STATE ROUTE	S	STEPS TO TRAIL
				4	MILE MARKER
				■	LANDMARK

TRAIL USE SYMBOLS

Black symbols: trail use allowed   Gray symbols: trail use not allowed

 Bicycling   Mountain Bicycling

 Hiking   In-line Skating

Bridal Path   Cross-Country Skiing

Handicap Accessible

XI

Ohio's Trails

Trail Name	Vicinity	Map Code	P.#
Bike & Hike Trail	Cleveland/Akron	RT-2	6
Blackhand Gorge Trail	Newark	RT-4	10
California Junction Trail	Cincinnati	ST-1	74
Celina-Coldwater Bikeway	Celina	RT-7	20
Darke County Park District Trail	Greenville	ST-5	75
Emerald Necklace Trail	Cleveland	BT-2	60
Evans Bike Trail, Thomas J.	Newark	RT-3	8
Gallipolis Bike Path	Gallipolis	RT-16	38
Gates Mills Trail	Cleveland	ST-4	75
Heritage Trail	Columbus	RT-18	44
Huffman Prairie Overlook Trail/ Kauffman Ave. Bike Path	Fairborn	RT-11	28
Huron Trail	Huron	ST-3	74
Interstate-480 Bikeway	Cleveland	BT-4	63
Interstate-670 Bikeway	Columbus	RT-12	30
Kokosing Gap Trail	Mount Vernon	RT-9	24
Little Miami Scenic Trail	Cincinnati/Springfield	RT-6	14
Marblehead Trail	Marblehead	ST-2	74
Miami & Erie Canal Towpath Trail	Toledo	BT-5	42
Nickelplate Trail	Louisville	RT-13	32
Oberlin Bikeway	Oberlin	RT-19	46
Ohio Canal Greenway	Newark	RT-10	26
Olentangy/ Lower Scioto Bikeways	Columbus	RT-1	2
Richland B. & O. Trail	Mansfield	RT-21	50
River Corridor Bikeway	Dayton	BT-1	54
Stavich Bicycle Trail	Youngstown	RT-5	12
Slippery Elm Trail	Bowling Green	RT-20	48
Towpath Trail	Cleveland/Akron	BT-3	68
University-Parks Hike-Bike Trail	Toledo	RT-15	36
Wabash Cannonball Trail	Toledo	RT-17	40
Wolf Creek Bikeway	Dayton	RT-14	34
Zane's Landing Trail	Zanesville	RT-8	22

OHIO'S TRAILS

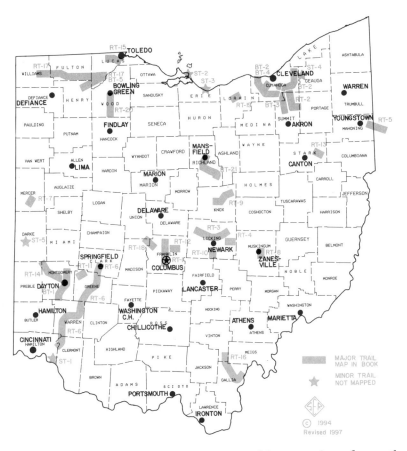

RT: Major Rail-Trail (greater than 1 mile and/or smooth surface trail following a former railroad).

BT: Bike Trail (smooth trail that does not follow a former railroad).

ST: Minor Rail-Trail (less than 1 mile and/or rough surface trail following a former railroad).

OHIO CHAMBERS OF COMMERCE

AKRON	216-376-5550		MIDDLEBURG HEIGHTS	216-243-5599
BEDFORD HEIGHTS	216-232-3369		MILFORD	513-831-2411
BELLVILLE	419-886-2245		MONTPELIER	419-485-4416
BEREA	216-243-8415		MORAINE	SEE KETTERING
BOWLING GREEN	419-353-7945		MORROW	513-899-4466
BRECKSVILLE	216-526-7350		MORROW	513-932-7185
BROADVIEW HEIGHTS	216-838-4510		MOUNT VERNON	614-393-1111
BROOKVILLE	513-833-2183		NEWARK	614-345-9757
BUCKEYE LAKE	614-928-8663		NORTH BALTIMORE	419-257-3523
BUTLER	SEE VANDALIA		NORTH OLMSTED	216-777-3368
CELINA	419-586-2219		NORTH ROYALTON	330-237-6180
CHAGRIN FALLS	216-247-6607		OAKWOOD	SEE KETTERING
CINCINNATI	513-579-3100		OBERLIN	216-774-6262
CLEVELAND	800-562-7121		PARMA	216-886-1700
COLDWATER	419-678-4881		PARMA HEIGHTS	SEE PARMA
COLUMBUS	614-221-1321		ROCKY RIVER	216-331-1140
CUYAHOGA FALLS	330-929-6756		SOLON	216-248-5080
DAYTON	513-226-1444		SOUTH METRO DAYTON	513-433-2032
DELTA	419-822-3089		SPRING VALLEY	513-862-4110
ELYRIA	SEE LORAIN		SPRINGFIELD	513-325-7621
FAIRBORN	513-878-0205		STOW	216-688-1579
GALLIPOLIS	614-446-0596		STRONGSVILLE	216-238-3366
GERMANTOWN	513-855-4121		SWANTON	419-826-1941
HILLIARD	614-876-7666		TOLEDO	419-243-8191
HUDSON	216-650-0621		TROTWOOD	513-837-1484
JOHNSTOWN	614-967-2334		VANDALIA	513-898-5351
KENT(KENT AREA)	330-673-9855		WATERVILLE	419-878-5188
KENT(BRIMFIELD)	330-678-1777		WAUSEON	419-335-9966
KETTERING	513-299-3852		WAYNESVILLE	513-897-8855
LAKEWOOD	216-226-2900		WEST CARROLLTON	SEE SOUTH METRO DAYTON
LEXINGTON	SEE MANSFIELD			
LORAIN	216-233-6500		WEST UNITY	419-924-2765
LOUISVILLE	216-875-7371		WORTHINGTON	614-888-3040
LOVELAND	513-683-1544		XENIA	513-372-3591
MANSFIELD	419-522-3211		YELLOW SPRINGS	513-767-2686
MAUMEE	419-893-5805		YOUNGSTOWN	330-744-2131
MIAMI TWP.	SEE MILFORD		ZANESVILLE	614-452-7571
MIAMISBURG	SEE SOUTH METRO DAYTON			

OHIO'S
MAJOR
RAIL-TRAILS

The Olentangy/Lower Scioto Bikeways

VICINITY: *Columbus*

TRAIL LENGTH: *18 miles (sections incomplete)*

SURFACE: *asphalt*

TRAIL USE:

Constructed in 1969, Ohio's first rail-trail, the Lower Scioto Bikeway, runs 1.5 miles between Frank Road and Greenlawn Avenue as it follows an abandoned railroad corridor along the west bank of the Scioto River. Bicyclists enter the south end of the bikeway from a fifty-foot dirt path accessible on Frank Road (S.R. 104). Although several sections of the trail remain to be constructed, the bikeway traverses Columbus from the south to the north end before proceeding north to Worthington. Many sections of Ohio's oldest trail suffer from outdated standards such as sharp curves, narrow bridges, and narrow urban sidewalks near Greenlawn Avenue. However, users will find most of the trail very scenic and pleasant to travel. Use extreme caution in congested areas.

Highlights along these trails include German Village, the State Capitol, Downtown Columbus, the *Santa Maria*, Ohio State University, Antrim Lake, and many scenic city parks. The most popular spot along the Olentangy Bikeway is the lake at Antrim Park, which offers wonderful scenery and a special loop trail around the lake for walkers and joggers. Another popular and scenic spot along the same trail is the Whetstone Park of Roses, where the trail can be tricky to follow. Study Map 2 closely to make sure you're headed in the right direction.

The City of Columbus Recreation and Parks Department has plans for extensions, connections, and improvements for the two bikeways in the near future. Contact them for current information.

PARKING:

Antrim Park offers the best spot to find a parking space along the trail, and parking is also available in the Whetstone Park of Roses.

FOR MORE INFORMATION:

City of Columbus Recreation & Parks Dept.
420 W. Whittier St. • Columbus, OH 43215
614-645-3308

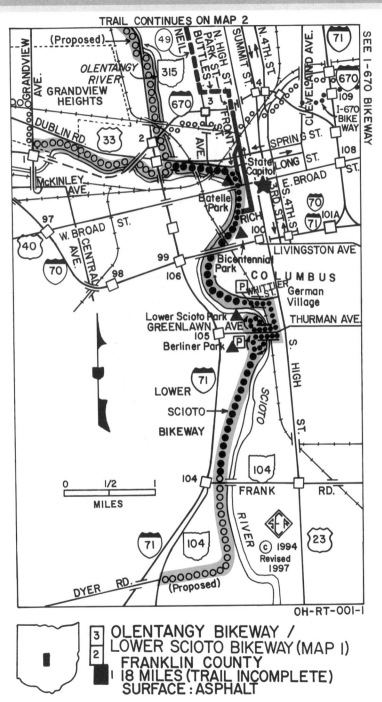

OH-RT-001-1

OLENTANGY BIKEWAY /
LOWER SCIOTO BIKEWAY (MAP 1)
FRANKLIN COUNTY
18 MILES (TRAIL INCOMPLETE)
SURFACE : ASPHALT

3

MAP 2 • OLENTANGY/LOWER SCIOTO BIKEWAYS

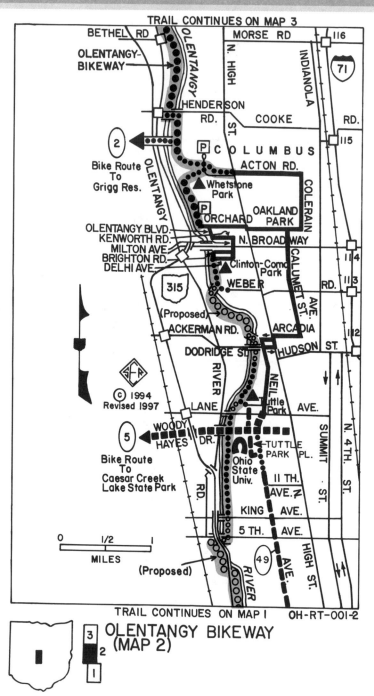

OLENTANGY BIKEWAY
(MAP 2)

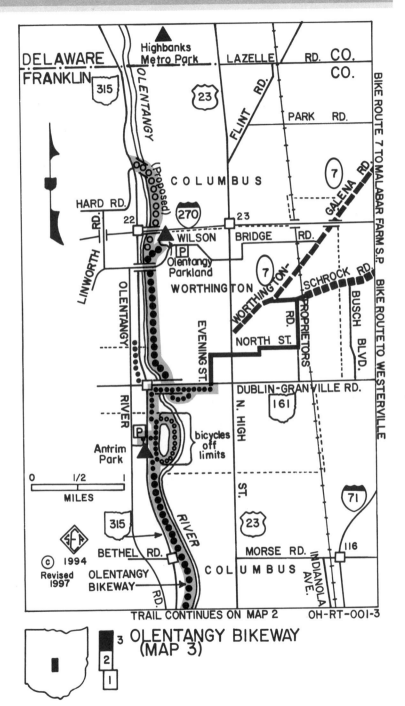

3 OLENTANGY BIKEWAY
(MAP 3)

BIKE AND HIKE TRAIL
VICINITY: *Cleveland/Akron*
TRAIL LENGTH: *29 miles*
SURFACE: *asphalt and smooth, crushed gravel*
TRAIL USE:

The Ohio Edison Company and the Metro Parks joined forces in 1972 to create the Bike and Hike Trail, and since that time Ohio's second rail-trail has been used as a model for similar efforts across the United States. Much of the path, which follows two old railroad grades and a former interurban electric railroad line, traverses the northern part of Summit County between Cleveland and Akron. Highlights include the Emerald Necklace, Brandywine Falls, Virginia Kendall Park (N.P.S.), Silver Springs Park and Campground, Crystal Lake, Silver Lake, Monroe Falls Metro Park, and the Cuyahoga River.

While most of the trail has a smooth, screened limestone surface, two sections have been covered with asphalt. The first of these paved paths parallels State Route 8 near Cuyahoga Falls while the second runs from Cuyahoga Falls to Kent. Streets marked with green and white "bike route" signs connect sections of the trail in Cuyahoga Falls. The most tranquil part of the trail lies between the Ohio Turnpike (Interstate-80) and State Route 303 where it runs through several deep railroad cuts with rock ledges on each side. Other spots along the trail have very high fills that provide trail users with a splendid view of the woods below.

This scenic trail connects with two other spectacular multipurpose trails, the Towpath Trail (page 68) to the west and, in the north, the Emerald Necklace Trail (page 60). Wheelchair users and bicyclists towing luggage trailers, take note: narrow entrances along the trail may hinder access; future construction plans call for wider entrances.

PARKING:
Parking is abundant along most of the trail.

FOR MORE INFORMATION:
Akron Metro Parks District
975 Treaty Line Rd. • Akron, OH 44313
216-867-5111

Cleveland Metro Parks
4101 Fulton Pkwy. • Cleveland, OH 44144
216-351-6300 Ext. 238

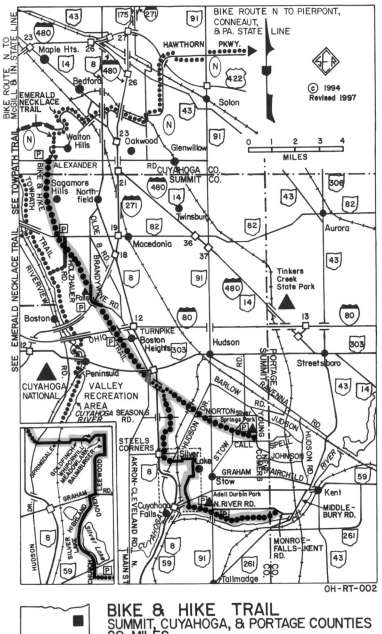

OH-RT-002

BIKE & HIKE TRAIL
SUMMIT, CUYAHOGA, & PORTAGE COUNTIES
29 MILES
SURFACE: SMOOTH CRUSHED GRAVEL &
ASPHALT

THOMAS J. EVANS BIKE TRAIL

VICINITY: *Newark*
TRAIL LENGTH: *14, 2.5, and 5.5 miles*
SURFACE: *asphalt*
TRAIL USE: 🚲 ⛷ 🚶 🦽 🐎 ⛷ ♿

Known as the Johnstown-Newark Bike Trail to many residents of Central Ohio, the Thomas J. Evans Bike Trail (West Segment) provides trail users with a great escape from the fast-paced lifestyle of Columbus. Most of this trail parallels Raccoon Creek through the Licking County countryside, offering users a variety of pastoral scenery, including farms, thick woods, colorful meadows, and long green canopies of trees.

Users enjoy flat and wooded terrain toward Johnstown, and a gradual five-mile decent provides an almost effortless ride from Johnstown to Alexandria. The trail scenery remains somewhat hilly beyond Alexandria before becoming very hilly near Newark.

Historic Granville, with its beautifully restored homes, old fashioned inns, boutiques, ice cream parlors, and Denison University, is a nice place to stop. The trail ends just west of Newark on Main Street, which riders can take east to reach downtown Newark.

East of downtown Newark's courthouse, along East Main Street, the Evans Bike Trail (East Segment) begins, just east of the North Fork Licking River (see Blackhand Gorge map, pg. 11). Known as the "Panhandle Trail," the trail parallels the Panhandle Line 5.5 miles from the North Licking River, in Newark, to the Licking Valley Road, near Hanover. Future plans include connecting all the east, middle and west segments of the Evans Bike Trail with the Blackhand Gorge trail and Ohio Canal Greenway.

PARKING:

Parking can be found in the cities of Johnstown, Alexandria, Newark, and Marne.

FOR MORE INFORMATION:
Thomas J. Evans Foundation
P.O. Box 4212 • Newark, OH 43055
614-349-3863

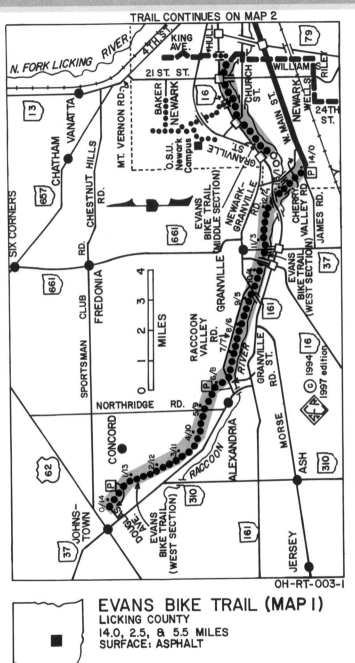

TRAIL CONTINUES ON MAP 2

OH-RT-003-1

EVANS BIKE TRAIL (MAP 1)
LICKING COUNTY
14.0, 2.5, & 5.5 MILES
SURFACE: ASPHALT

BLACKHAND GORGE TRAIL

VICINITY: *Newark*

TRAIL LENGTH: *5.5 miles*

SURFACE: *asphalt (4.5 m.); dirt & gravel (1m.)*

TRAIL USE:

The Ohio-to-Erie Canal, Central Ohio Railroad, and interurban electric lines near Newark were abandoned in 1929, and only traces of them can be found today. The area in which they once lay, however, was revitalized in 1975 with the dedication of the Blackhand Gorge State Nature Preserve. The preserve—created for scientific, educational, aesthetic, and recreational opportunities—takes its name from the narrow east-west chasm the Licking River cuts through the preserve's sandstone formation. It also plays host to the Blackhand Gorge Trail, one of Ohio's most spectacular rail-trails.

While the main section of the Blackhand Gorge Trail is a paved bike path running along the former Central Ohio Railroad, all types of trail users can enjoy this wonderful 4.5-mile trail. Its east end clearly displays the rock exposed as workers cut a path for the old railroad. A separate scenic section open to walkers and hikers follows the former interurban electric line for one mile over dirt and gravel and through a tunnel. Many other dirt paths connect with the main Blackhand Gorge Trail, offering hikers an opportunity to further explore the scenic valley.

Future considerations include connecting this trail to Newark and to the Thomas J. Evans Bike Trail (page 8). For more information, write to the address below.

PARKING:

Parking can be found at each end of the trail.

FOR MORE INFORMATION:

Ohio Dept. of Natural Resources
Fountain Square • Columbus, OH 43224
614-265-6395

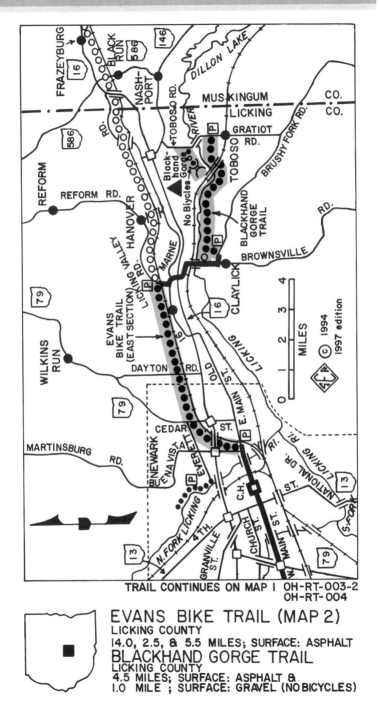

TRAIL CONTINUES ON MAP 1   OH-RT-003-2
OH-RT-004

EVANS BIKE TRAIL (MAP 2)
LICKING COUNTY
14.0, 2.5, & 5.5 MILES; SURFACE: ASPHALT

BLACKHAND GORGE TRAIL
LICKING COUNTY
4.5 MILES; SURFACE: ASPHALT &
1.0 MILE ; SURFACE: GRAVEL (NO BICYCLES)

11

STAVICH BICYCLE TRAIL

VICINITY: *Youngstown*
TRAIL LENGTH: *11 miles*
SURFACE: *asphalt*

TRAIL USE: 🚴 🚵 🚶 🛏 🐕 ⛷ ♿

The Stavich Bicycle Trail opened in 1983 and follows a former inter-urban electric railroad grade through three townships, two counties, and even a second state. The trail, constructed and maintained by the families of John and George Stavich, follows the Mahoning River from Struthers, Ohio, to New Castle, Pennsylvania, offering users a vast variety of scenery, including green rolling hills, farmlands, and wooded hillsides.

PARKING:

Parking can be found in Struthers along State Route 289 just east of State Route 616 and along Liberty Street in Lowellville where the trail runs for seven blocks.

FOR MORE INFORMATION:

Falcon Foundry, 6th. & Water Streets
P.O. Box 301 • Lowellville, OH 44436
216-536-6221

The 11-mile Stavich Bicycle Trail Parallels the B. & O. Railroad.

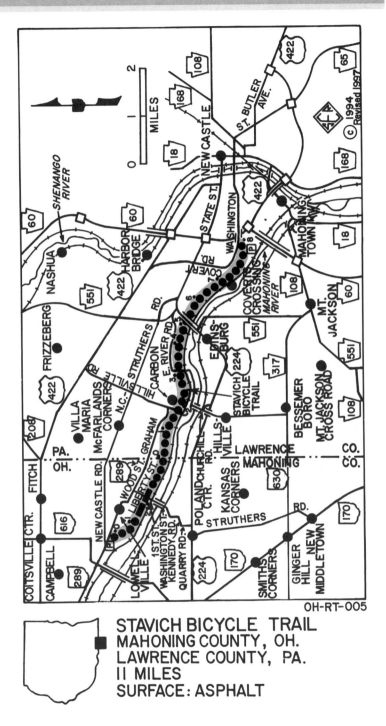

OH-RT-005

STAVICH BICYCLE TRAIL
MAHONING COUNTY, OH.
LAWRENCE COUNTY, PA.
II MILES
SURFACE: ASPHALT

13

LITTLE MIAMI SCENIC TRAIL

VICINITY: *Cincinnati-Springfield*

TRAIL LENGTH: *72 miles (entire trail; sections incomplete)*
Milford-Xenia: 50 miles
Xenia-Yellow Springs: 10 miles
Springfield: 3 miles

SURFACE: *asphalt with parallel dirt surface*

TRAIL USE:

With 72 miles winding along the Little Miami River through much of Southwestern Ohio, the Little Miami Scenic Trail is the longest rail-trail in the Buckeye State. The trail starts from its south end near Mariemont at Kroger Hill and runs through Terrace Park, Milford, Miamiville, Loveland, South Lebanon, Morrow, Fort Ancient State Park, Mathers Mills, Oregonia, Corwin, Roxanna, Spring Valley, Xenia, Yellow Springs, Emery Chapel, and Beatty before reaching its north end at Springfield.

Two sections of the trail offer both asphalt and a paralleling dirt path for horseback riders. The first section runs 50 miles from Milford to Xenia, and is managed by both the Little Miami Scenic State Park and the Greene County Park District. The second section runs 10-miles from Xenia to Yellow Springs and is managed by the Greene County Park District.

A third section of the trail, about 3 miles in Springfield, has been surfaced with asphalt but does not include a bridal path. Future plans include surfacing more sections with asphalt and adding a parallel dirt trail for all trail users. Contact the Springfield Parks and Recreation Department for information on this portion of the trail.

The trail follows the meandering Little Miami River through Hamilton, Clermont, Warren, and Southern Greene Counties, offering users views of rolling farm country, small cliffs, and steep gorges with outcropping rocks. Other sights include a deep forested valley with steep hillsides, some with high bridges crossing the valley. The Little Miami River Valley is rich with the history and burial grounds of Native Americans, and battles of the Revolutionary War and the French and Indian War were fought here. During the first and second

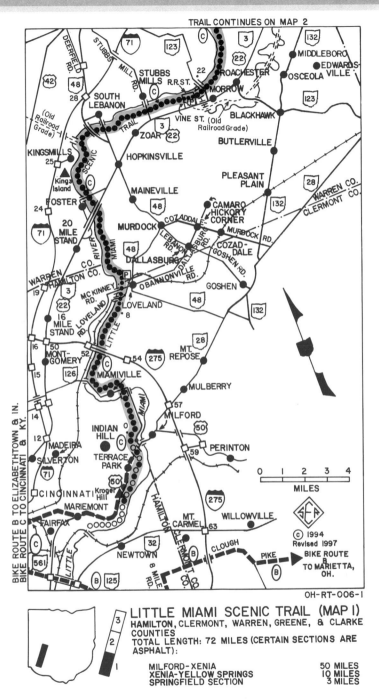

TRAIL CONTINUES ON MAP 2

OH-RT-006-1

LITTLE MIAMI SCENIC TRAIL (MAP 1)
HAMILTON, CLERMONT, WARREN, GREENE, & CLARKE COUNTIES
TOTAL LENGTH: 72 MILES (CERTAIN SECTIONS ARE ASPHALT):

MILFORD-XENIA	50 MILES
XENIA-YELLOW SPRINGS	10 MILES
SPRINGFIELD SECTION	3 MILES

world wars, the railroad line that the trail now follows once helped transport ammunition manufactured at the Peters' Cartridge Company in Kings Mills.

As the trail travels through most of Greene County, it leaves the banks of the Little Miami to run through the towns of Spring Valley, Xenia, and Yellow Springs, utilizing a steel bridge to span the river between Xenia and Yellow Springs. While much of the Greene County scenery consists of farmlands and green shady woods, the Xenia to Yellow Springs section of the trail offers highlights such as the Greene County Court House, Shawnee Park, John Bryan State Park, Glen Helen Nature Preserve, and Antioch College.

While most of Clarke County's portion of the trail between Yellow Springs and Springfield has yet to be developed, the three miles from John Street to Center Street in Springfield, which make up the very north end of the rail-trail, have been surfaced with asphalt.

Future plans for the Little Miami Scenic Trail include many extensions. From Kroger Hill, the trail will extend south to connect with planned and existing bikeways in Cincinnati. Since Xenia was once a railroad hub, plans have been developed to link the Little Miami Scenic Trail with other trails at Xenia's Barrs Bottom. To the west, the H-Connector

A shady stretch of the Little Miami Scenic Trail between Loveland and Morrow.

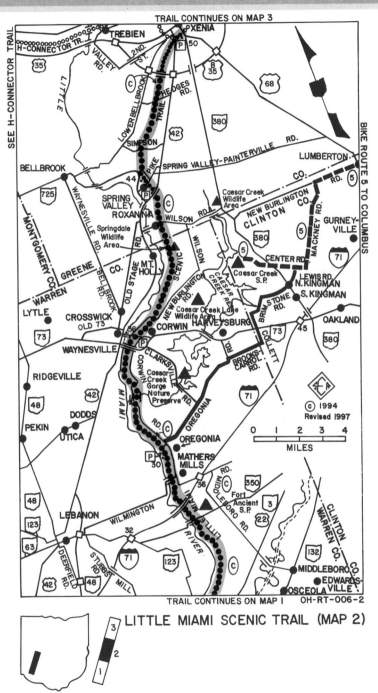

LITTLE MIAMI SCENIC TRAIL (MAP 2)

Horseback riders can enjoy the dirt path paralleling the asphalt trail.

Trail will connect Xenia with Dayton and the River Corridor Bikeway (Page 54). In the Northeast, the Ohio-to-Erie Trail is planned to connect Xenia to Columbus and Cleveland using both abandoned railroads and canals. To the southeast, the Jamestown Bikeway will connect Xenia to Jamestown. For current information contact the addresses below.

PARKING:

Parking can be found in Miamiville, Loveland, Morrow, Oregonia, Corwin, Spring Valley, Xenia, and Yellow Springs.

FOR MORE INFORMATION:

State Park Section (southern)
Little Miami Scenic State Park
8570 E.S.R. 73 • Waynesville, OH 45068
513-897-3055

Clark County Section (northern)
Springfield Parks & Recreation, City Hall
76 E. High St. • Springfield, OH 45502
513-324-7348

Green County Section (central)
Green County Park District
651 Dayton-Xenia Rd. • Xenia, OH 45385
513-376-7440

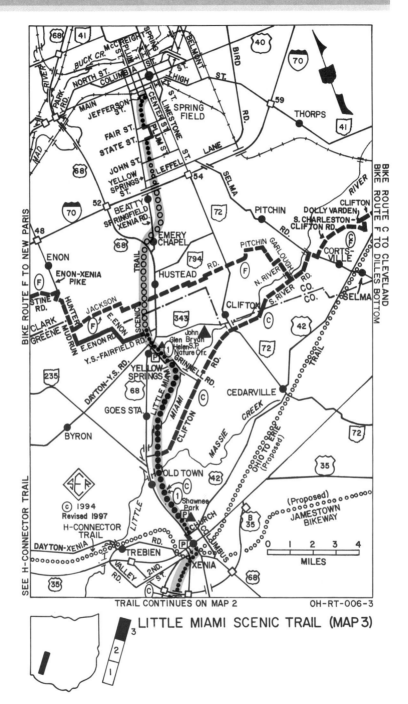

LITTLE MIAMI SCENIC TRAIL (MAP 3)

TRAIL CONTINUES ON MAP 2

OH-RT-006-3

CELINA-COLDWATER BIKEWAY

VICINITY: *Celina*
TRAIL LENGTH: *4.5 miles*
SURFACE: *asphalt*
TRAIL USE:

The 4.5 miles of the Celina-Coldwater Bikeway connects Celina to Coldwater and parallels an active railroad. Well received by both communities it serves, the trail is used by local residents for commuting, socializing, and recreating. The trail's scenic rural atmosphere has encouraged many families to enjoy their natural surroundings.

Most of the scenery consists of farmlands, but the main attraction is Grand Lake Saint Mary's, once the largest man-made lake in the world. The Huffy Bicycle Company, headquartered in Celina, purchased the old railroad right-of-way through the Huffy Foundation. Celina, with the help of the Ohio Department of Transportation, secured the construction grant to build the bikeway.

PARKING:
Parking is available in Celina at the corner of Schunk and U.S. 127.

From left: *Author Shawn Richardson, Steve Slucher, and Tom Boone get ready to ride.*

FOR MORE INFORMATION:
Celina Engineering Dept.
426 W. Market • Celina, OH 45822
419-586-1144

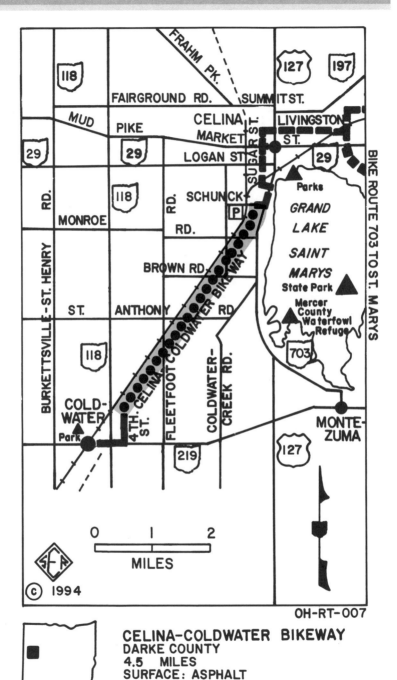

OH-RT-007

CELINA-COLDWATER BIKEWAY
DARKE COUNTY
4.5 MILES
SURFACE: ASPHALT

21

ZANE'S LANDING TRAIL
VICINITY: *Zanesville*
TRAIL LENGTH: *3 miles*
SURFACE: *asphalt*
TRAIL USE:

The 3 miles of the Zane's Landing Trail take trail users from Market Street in Downtown Zanesville to Riverview Park in the city's north end. A safety barrier separates the rail-trail from the active railroad it parallels as it follows the Muskingum River north under Interstate 70 to connect with various parks along the river front.

Attractions along the trail include a restored train depot on Market Street near the path's south entrance. The *Lorena*, a paddle boat that runs up and down the Muskingum River alongside the bike path, also docks nearby. Zanesville's famous Y-Bridge crosses the Muskingum and Licking Rivers just three blocks south of the old train depot at Main Street (U.S. 40).

PARKING:
Trail users can park at the lot next to the trail access at Market Street in Downtown Zanesville. Parking is also available along the bikeway as users near Riverview Park along the Muskingum River about a mile before the trail ends.

FOR MORE INFORMATION:
City of Zanesville
401 Market St. • Zanesville, OH 43701
614-455-0609

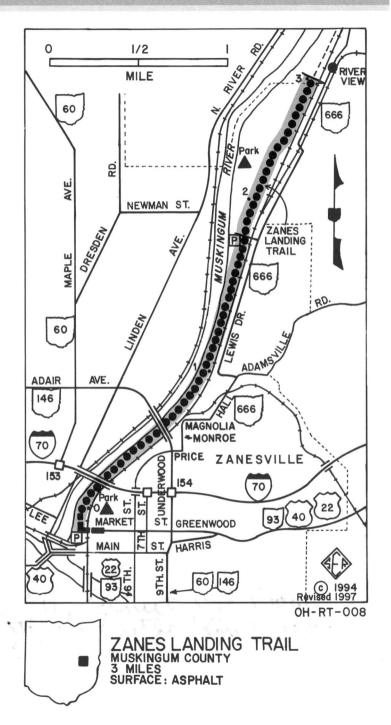

OH-RT-008

ZANES LANDING TRAIL
MUSKINGUM COUNTY
3 MILES
SURFACE: ASPHALT

23

KOKOSING GAP TRAIL

VICINITY: *Mount Vernon*
TRAIL LENGTH: *13.2 miles*
SURFACE: *asphalt*
TRAIL USE: 🚴 🛴 🚶 🏕 🐕 ⛷ ♿

Converted from the old Pennsylvania Railroad, the Kokosing Gap Trail opened to the public in October, 1991. The trail crosses the Kokosing River twice over two steel span bridges, and mile markers have been established along the trail to help users compute distances traveled from Mount Vernon. Much of the trail runs through forested hills along the Kokosing River while other scenery includes wetlands, family farms, and villages.

A parking lot southeast of downtown Mount Vernon along Mount Vernon Avenue provides access to the start of the trail. From Phillips Park the trail takes users east to historic Gambier, home of Kenyon College and many fine antique stores, shops, and boutiques.

The trail continues northeast from Gambier to Howard, where it passes under U.S. Highway 36 through a spectacular stone arch tunnel. From Howard, the trail proceeds to Danville, where users can take advantage of the town's many fine restaurants and specialty shops.

Future plans for the Kokosing Gap Trail involve extending it east from Danville along the same former railroad grade to hook up with another rails-to-trails project in Holmes County. The new stretch of trail will take the users through Amish country. For current information, write to the address below.

PARKING:
Besides the Mount Vernon and Gambier access lots, users can park along the trail off Highway 36 in Howard and in Danville at the trail's access on Washington Street near Highway 62.

on Newark Rd turn on Mt.
Vernon right after Rite Aid
Drug on left.

FOR MORE INFORMATION:
Kokosing Gap Trail
P.O. Box 129 • *Gambier, OH 43022*
614-427-4509 or 614-587-6267

24

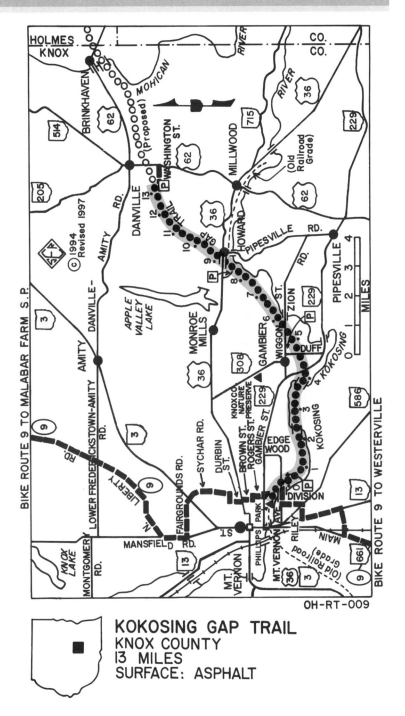

OH-RT-009

KOKOSING GAP TRAIL
KNOX COUNTY
13 MILES
SURFACE: ASPHALT

25

Ohio Canal Greenway

VICINITY: *Newark*
TRAIL LENGTH: *3 miles*
SURFACE: *original ballast*

TRAIL USE:

The Ohio Canal Greenway utilizes both an old rail line and the tow-path of the old Ohio-Erie Canal. The trail starts in the center of Hebron on U.S. 40 and runs past the town's Canal Park where it picks up and follows the old canal for three miles to State Route 79 on the Fairfield-Licking County Line. A replica of a covered bridge crosses a small stream near the Interstate-70 underpass. From the south end of the trail, users can travel State Route 360 southeast to Buckeye Lake.

Future plans include a smoother surface for the trail so all types of users can enjoy it. Considerations are being made to extend the trail to connect it with the Thomas J. Evans Bike Trail (West Segment, see page 8) and to a planned rails-to-trails project in Perry County.

PARKING:
There are currently no designated parking areas for this trail.

A replica covered bridge takes Ohio Canal Greenway users across a small stream.

FOR MORE INFORMATION:
Licking County Park District
4309 Lancaster Rd. • Granville, OH 43023
614-587-2535

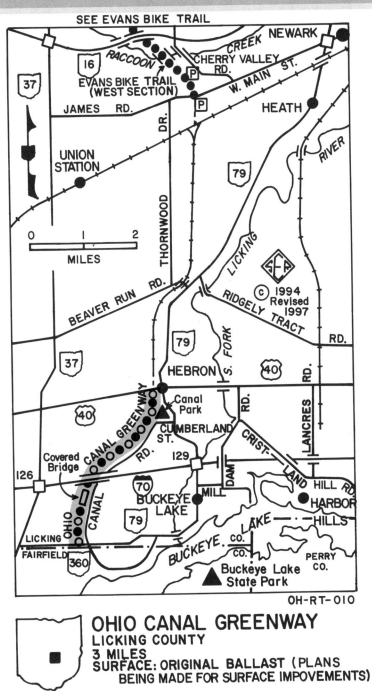

SEE EVANS BIKE TRAIL

CREEK NEWARK

16

RACCOON

CHERRY VALLEY RD.

37

EVANS BIKE TRAIL
(WEST SECTION)

W. MAIN ST.

JAMES RD.

HEATH

UNION
STATION

THORNWOOD DR.

79

RIVER

LICKING

0   1   2

MILES

BEAVER RUN RD.

RIDGELY TRACT

© 1994
Revised
1997

RD.

79

S. FORK

37

HEBRON

40

RD.

CANAL GREENWAY

Canal
Park

40

CUMBERLAND
ST.

RD.

CRIST-LAND

LANCRES RD.

Covered
Bridge

RD.

129

DAM

HILL RD.

126

70

BUCKEYE
LAKE

MILL

HARBOR

79

LAKE

HILLS

OHIO CANAL

LICKING

BUCKEYE

CO. LAKE

PERRY
CO.

FAIRFIELD

360

CO.

Buckeye Lake
State Park

OH-RT-010

OHIO CANAL GREENWAY
LICKING COUNTY
3 MILES
SURFACE: ORIGINAL BALLAST (PLANS
BEING MADE FOR SURFACE IMPOVEMENTS)

HUFFMAN PRAIRIE OVERLOOK TRAIL

VICINITY: *Fairborn*
TRAIL LENGTH: *5 miles*
SURFACE: *original ballast*
TRAIL USE:

The Huffman Prairie Overlook Trail follows two different abandoned railroad grades and parallels an active railroad. The rail-trail also runs alongside the Kauffman Avenue Bike Path, a 2-mile stretch of concrete open to bicyclists, mountain bicyclists, walkers, and wheelchair users. Both paths have been incorporated in the Miami Valley Regional Bicycle Committee's plans for a larger trail project that will eventually link up to the Dayton Bikeway System.

Finding the Huffman Prairie Overlook Trail near the site of the Wright Brothers Memorial (the intersection of State Route 444 and Kauffman Avenue) may be tricky at times, as the area is susceptible to tree over-growth. The rail-trail follows the north levy of the active railroad, which keeps trail users a safe distance from the trains. The trail passes the north edge of Wright State University near the intersection of Colonel Glenn Highway and Kauffman Avenue.

Although both the Huffman Prairie Overlook Trail and the Kauffman Avenue Bike Path are in the early stages of development, they will eventually form a very important link to the greenway trail network throughout Ohio. For more information on the progress of these trails, contact the the Miami Valley Regional Bicycle Committee at the address below.

PARKING:
Parking can be found at the Wright Brothers' Memorial toward the west end of the trail off of Kauffman Avenue.

FOR MORE INFORMATION:
Miami Valley Regional Bicycle Committee
1304 Horizon Dr. • Fairborn, OH 45324
513-879-2068 or 513-255-4097

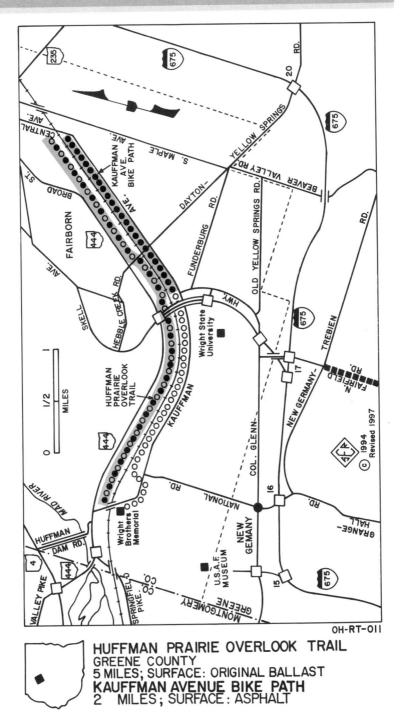

OH-RT-OII

HUFFMAN PRAIRIE OVERLOOK TRAIL
GREENE COUNTY
5 MILES; SURFACE: ORIGINAL BALLAST
KAUFFMAN AVENUE BIKE PATH
2 MILES; SURFACE: ASPHALT

29

INTERSTATE-670 BIKEWAY
VICINITY: *Columbus*
TRAIL LENGTH: *3 miles*
SURFACE: *asphalt*
TRAIL USE:

Until the late 1980s, a very large section of Columbus northeast of the State Capitol building teemed with railroad activity. The former railroad yard has since been transformed to include new streets, interstate Highway 670, and its own rail-trail, the I-670 Bikeway. Only one active Conrail line remains.

The three miles of asphalt that make up the I-670 Bikeway stretch from Cleveland Avenue to Airport Avenue. Future considerations include both an east and west extension to connect the trail to the Olentangy-Scioto Bikeway and to the future Alum Creek Bikeway. The I-670 Bikeway may also become part of the Ohio-Erie Trail, allowing users to travel from Cincinnati to Columbus to Cleveland.

PARKING:
There are currently no designated parking areas for this trail.

FOR MORE INFORMATION:
City of Columbus, Division of Traffic Engineering
109 N. Front St. • Columbus, OH 43215
614-645-7790

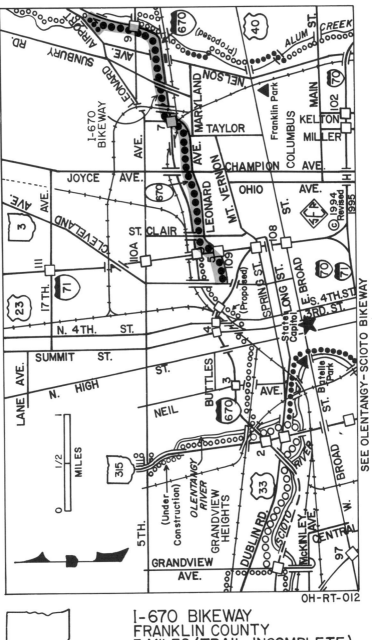

OH-RT-012

I-670 BIKEWAY
FRANKLIN COUNTY
3 MILES (TRAIL INCOMPLETE)
SURFACE: ASPHALT

NICKELPLATE TRAIL

VICINITY: *Louisville*

TRAIL LENGTH: *2.5 miles*

SURFACE: *asphalt*

TRAIL USE:

The 88 acres of Metzgar Park were donated to the City of Louisville by Mary C. Metzger, whose will stated that the land should be used as a park. The 1.5 miles of asphalt paved rail-trail that forms the Nickelplate Trail runs past Metzger Park diagonally from northwest to southeast. The trail also connects with a network of smaller asphalt paths in the park to create a total of 2.5 miles of smoothly surfaced trail.

Scenery along the Nickelplate Trail consists mostly of meadows and woods, and the tranquil trail is dotted with benches for users to stop and enjoy the sounds of nature. Future plans for the park include adding recreation fields and possibly extending the Nickelplate Trail to the southeast.

PARKING:

A parking lot at the trail's southeast entrance next to Dellbrook Avenue provides the most convenient parking, but a larger lot is located inside Metzgar Park just off of Nickelplate Avenue south of Edmar Street.

FOR MORE INFORMATION:

Nickelplate Trail

215 S. Mill St. • Louisville, OH 44641

216-875-3321

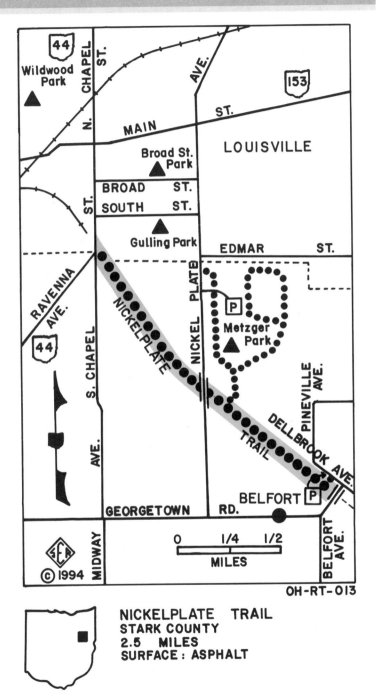

NICKELPLATE TRAIL
STARK COUNTY
2.5 MILES
SURFACE: ASPHALT

OH-RT-013

33

WOLF CREEK BIKEWAY

VICINITY: *Dayton*
TRAIL LENGTH: *13 miles*
SURFACE: *smooth crushed gravel*
TRAIL USE: 🚲 🚵 🏃 🛏 🐾 ⛷ ♿

The Wolf Creek Bikeway offers Dayton-area residents a rural alterna-tive to the River Corridor Bikeway (page 54). Currently 13 miles of smooth crushed gravel, the trail follows the old CSX railroad grade from just west of Dayton on Olive Road and runs northwest to Verona on the Montgomery-Preble County Line.

The trail runs through a relatively flat section of Montgomery County where colorful woods, picturesque meadows, and family farms make it a very scenic route. Users may wish to stop off in Trotwood to have a bite at local restaurants or visit the preserved train depot to see its display of old cabooses. Trail users can even camp at Sycamore State Park, the most scenic part of the trail. Further up the trail, Brookville plays host to a second preserved depot as well as many fine shops, restaurants, and Golden Gate Park. From Brookville, the trail continues under Interstate-70 and on up through the countryside to Dodson, Bachman, Wengerlawn, and Verona.

Possible future plans for the Wolf Creek Bikeway include expanding the trail in both directions. One idea extends the trail from Olive Road southeast into Dayton to connect with the James McGee Boulevard Bikeway and the River Corridor Bikeway (page 54). Another plan involves extending the trail northwest from Verona to Greenville. For current information write to the address below.

PARKING:
Parking for this trail can be found along the streets of Trotwood and Brookville.

FOR MORE INFORMATION:
Park District of Dayton-Montgomery County
1375 E. Siebenthaler Ave. • Dayton, OH 45414
513-275-7275

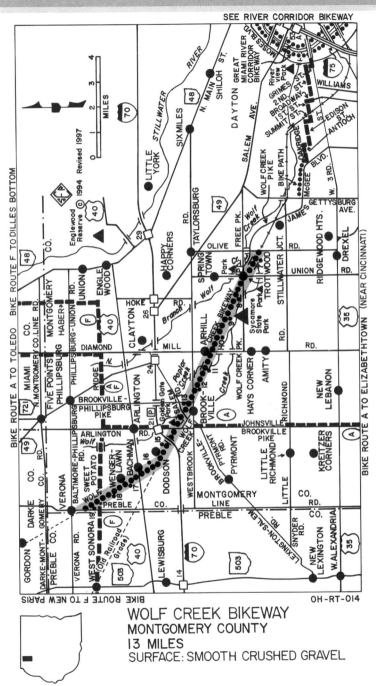

WOLF CREEK BIKEWAY
MONTGOMERY COUNTY
13 MILES
SURFACE: SMOOTH CRUSHED GRAVEL

OH-RT-014

UNIVERSITY-PARK HIKE-BIKE TRAIL

VICINITY: *Toledo*
TRAIL LENGTH: *6.3 miles*
SURFACE: *asphalt*
TRAIL USE:

Even before workers paved the University-Park Hike-Bike Trail, mountain bicyclists and hikers in western Toledo used the path extensively. The six-mile asphalt trail starts at Toledo's west end on King Road between Central Avenue and Sylvania Avenue near Milton Olander Park and runs east to the University of Toledo campus.

From King Road the trail goes east under Interstate-475 and U.S. 23 before reaching Sylvania Road where it curves and intersects with another trail leading into Wildwood Preserve Metro Park. The Metro Park offers users a variety of recreational activities as well as many scenic foot paths and a loop bicycle trail. Past the Metro Park, the trail crosses two bridges over Central Avenue and Secor Road on its way to the University of Toledo Campus. This section of the trail parallels an active railroad, but a thicket of trees separate the two paths so well users may hardly even notice the railroad.

While the rail-trail currently ends at the University of Toledo Campus, future plans include connecting it to a nearby network of bike trails that run through Ottawa Park, Jermain Parks, and the University of Toledo Scott Park campus. For current information contact the address below.

PARKING:
Parking for this trail can be found in Wildwood Preserve Metro Park.

FOR MORE INFORMATION:
Toledo Area Metro parks
5100 W. Central, Toledo • *OH 43615*
419-535-3050

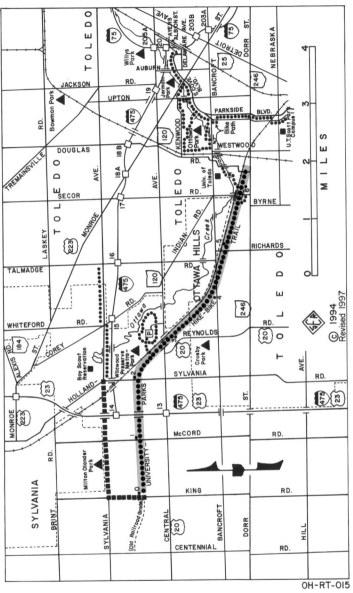

OH-RT-015

UNIVERSITY—PARK HIKE-BIKE TRAIL
LUCAS COUNTY
6 MILES
TRAIL SURFACE: ASPHALT

GALLIPOLIS BIKE PATH

VICINITY: *Gallipolis*
TRAIL LENGTH: *2.5 & 4.5 miles*
SURFACE: *smooth crushed gravel*
TRAIL USE:

The Gallipolis Bike Path runs through a very scenic and mountainous part of the Buckeye State. The town of Gallipolis is across the Ohio River from West Virginia. The two developed trail sections form just a small part of the planned 25-mile cross-state trail, which will eventually run from Kanauga to Gallipolis then north to Vinton and Minerton. While most of the surrounding terrain is mountainous, the trail runs through deep cuts and high fills, making it a relatively flat and spectacular journey for cyclists and hikers. Future plans include surfacing the entire trail with asphalt.

Settled by French immigrants in 1790, Gallipolis is one of southern Ohio's most picturesque historical towns. Trail users can follow side streets seven blocks to the town's center. where its main park faces the Ohio River and features a restored 1878 bandstand. Gallipolis also offers trail users several restaurants to stop and enjoy a bite in the east end of town.

PARKING:
Parking for this trail can be found along the streets of Gallipolis, Kerr, and Bidwell.

FOR MORE INFORMATION:
O. O. McIntyre Park District
Gallia County Court House • Gallipolis, OH 45631
614-446-4612

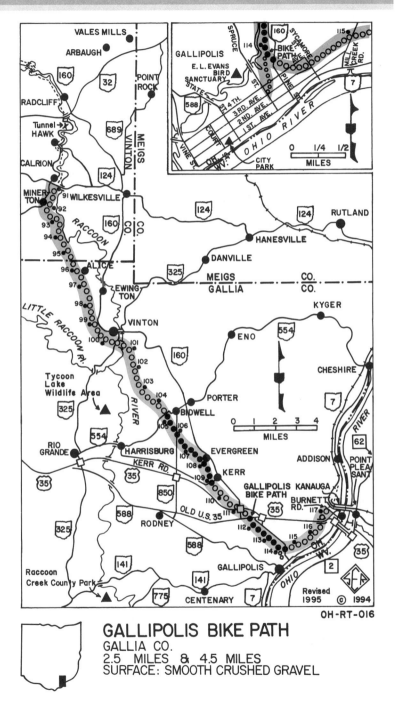

OH-RT-016

GALLIPOLIS BIKE PATH
GALLIA CO.
2.5 MILES & 4.5 MILES
SURFACE: SMOOTH CRUSHED GRAVEL

WABASH CANNONBALL TRAIL

VICINITY: *Toledo*

TRAIL LENGTH: *65 miles*

SURFACE: *undeveloped (3.5 miles in Oak Openings Preserve*
Metro Park contains a smooth crushed gravel surface)

TRAIL USE:

Second in length only to the Little Miami Scenic Trail (page 14), the 65-mile Wabash Cannonball Trail promises to become a wonderful recreational resource to residents and visitors of Toledo and Northwestern Ohio. A great deal of development, however, still awaits the new trail. So far, only 3.5 miles of the trail in Lucas County contain a smooth crushed limestone surface. The developed corridor runs from State Route 295 through the Oak Openings Preserve Metro Park to the Lucas-Fulton County Line.

Near future plans for the Wabash Cannonball Trail include continuing the clearing and regrading process along undeveloped sections. Long range plans involve linking the trail with local bike paths in Maumee and to the North Inland Coast Trail, the Slippery Elm Trail (page 48),

The Maumee River parallels the 10.5-mile Miami & Erie Canal towpath, which is described along with the Wabash Cannonball Trail on the next page.

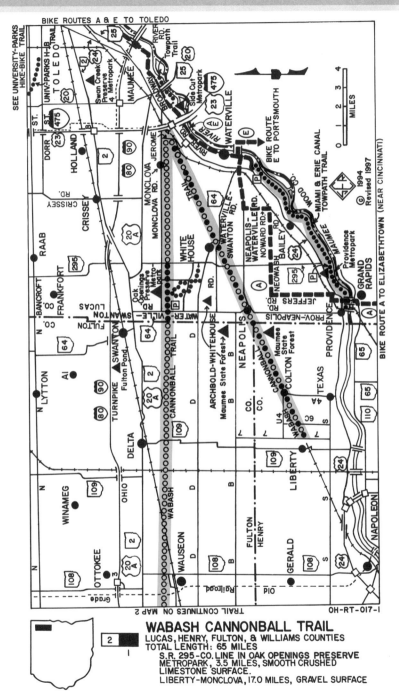

WABASH CANNONBALL TRAIL

LUCAS, HENRY, FULTON, & WILLIAMS COUNTIES
TOTAL LENGTH: 65 MILES

S.R. 295-CO. LINE IN OAK OPENINGS PRESERVE
METROPARK, 3.5 MILES, SMOOTH CRUSHED
LIMESTONE SURFACE.
LIBERTY-MONCLOVA, 17.0 MILES, GRAVEL SURFACE

OH-RT-017-I

and the Miami & Erie Canal Towpath Trail, providing Northwest Ohio with a major network of greenways.

Most of the Miami & Erie Canal Towpath Trail runs 10.1 miles through wooded areas between the old canal bed and the Scenic Maumee River from Providence to Waterville. Trail users will enjoy stopping along the path's smooth gravel and concrete surface between the town of Providence and Providence Metro Park, where they can watch mules pulling a restored canal barge along the old towpath. Between Providence Metro Park and Farnsworth Metro Park, the trail surface shifts to a smooth-to-moderate dirt surface that closes to all bicycles and mountain bicycles from January to March and other periods of wet weather (although this dirt section of the the trail allows for standard touring bicycles, mountain bicycles provide easier navigation of its mild bumpy spots). The remainder of the trail, from Farnsworth Metro Park to the edge of Waterville, provides users with a smooth gravel and asphalt surface.

For more information about the Miami & Erie Canal Towpath Trail, write to the Metro Parks Administrative Offices, 5100 West Central Avenue, Toldeo, Ohio 43615, or call 419-535-3050. If you need additional information concerning the Wabash Cannonball Trail, write to the address below.

PARKING:
At this time, parking can be found in Oak Openings Preserve Metro Park on State Route 64.

FOR MORE INFORMATION:
NORTA, Inc. (Northwestern Ohio Rails-to-Trails Association, Inc.)
P. O. Box 234 • Delta, OH 43515
1-800-951-4788

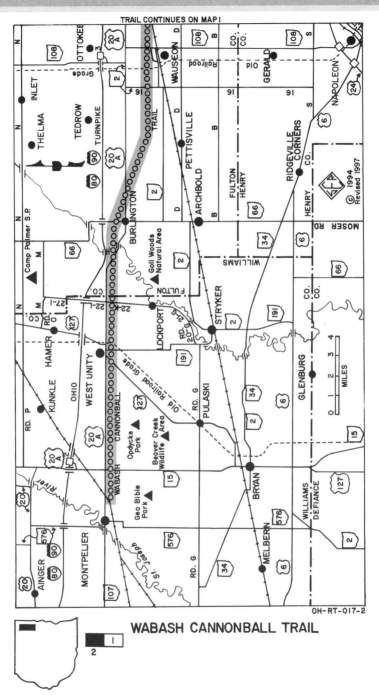

TRAIL CONTINUES ON MAP I

WABASH CANNONBALL TRAIL

OH-RT-017-2

43

HERITAGE TRAIL

VICINITY: *Columbus*
TRAIL LENGTH: *7.5 miles*
SURFACE: *undeveloped (asphalt covers 2.5 miles in Hilliard)*
TRAIL USE:

The Heritage Trail provides users in the Northwest area of Columbus and Franklin County with a great recreational opportunity. The trail starts in a center section of Hilliard known as Old Hilliard, where historical buildings, brick sidewalks, and old-fashioned street lamps line Main Street. From there the trail travels northwest through a rural midwest landscape toward Homestead Park, which offers users a variety of recreational facilities including shelter for outings, elaborate playgrounds, and a circular recreation trail adjacent to the Heritage Trail.

Future plans for the trail include developing it from Homestead Park to Plain City, which would expand the entire trail to 7.5 miles. Spacious farms and fields make up much of the trail's scenery while several areas of woodland dot the countryside near Madison County. A stone arch trestle built in 1901 crosses over Sugar Run and a concrete trestle crosses over the Darby River into Plain City on the Madison-Union County line, where trail users can enjoy a meal at one of two great Amish restaurants on US-42 south of Plain City. (Note: Between Cemetery Pike and Plain City, the trail is still in private ownership).

PARKING:
Parking for this trail is available in the center of Old Hilliard and at Homestead Park on Cosgray Road.

FOR MORE INFORMATION:
Heritage Rails-to-Trails Coalition • c/o Homestead Park
4675 Cosgray Rd. • Amlin, OH 43002
614-876-9554

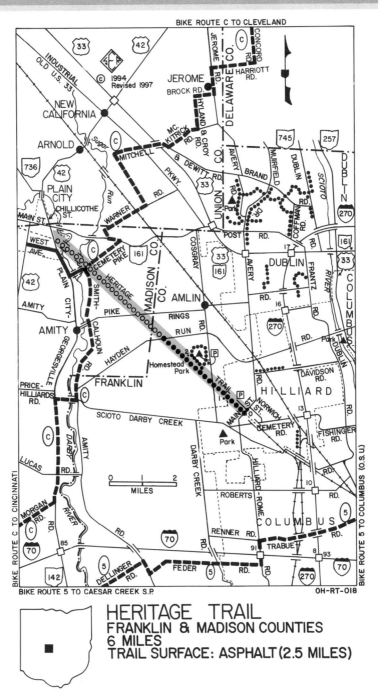

BIKE ROUTE C TO CLEVELAND

© 1994 Revised 1997

HERITAGE TRAIL
FRANKLIN & MADISON COUNTIES
6 MILES
TRAIL SURFACE: ASPHALT (2.5 MILES)

OH-RT-018

BIKE ROUTE 5 TO CAESAR CREEK S.P.

45

OBERLIN BIKEWAY

VICINITY: *Oberlin*

TRAIL LENGTH: *2.8 miles*

SURFACE: *asphalt*

TRAIL USE:

The 2.8-mile Oberlin Bikeway runs straight through Oberlin along the former Conrail Line from Pyle-South Amherst Road to Oberlin Road. Like many towns in Ohio, Oberlin shares a history of railroads that no longer exist. Oberlin, however, is more famous for a former railroad that never needed a developed grade: the Underground Railroad.

The Underground Railroad, of course, was the trail Harriet Tubman and other abolitionists used to help slaves escape from southern and border states to the north during the nineteenth century. Oberlin was the last stop along the Underground Railroad before fugitive slaves crossed Lake Erie into Canada. Many former slaves, however, stayed to make Oberlin their home. Today, the town's art, shops, and multicultural events reflect its rich history of African-American culture. Trail enthusiasts may wish to time their journey on the Oberlin Bikeway to coincide with the town's annual summer Afro-American festival.

The Oberlin Bikeway is actually the first phase of a planned 12-mile bike path designed to create an east-west corridor through Lorain County. The entire trail will follow the former railroad right-of-way from Kipton through Oberlin to Elyria and may also become part of the proposed North Inland Coast Trail.

PARKING:

Parking for this trail can be found at the former depot on State Route 58 in Oberlin.

FOR MORE INFORMATION:

Lorain County Park District

85 S. Main St • Oberlin, OH 44074

216-775-1513

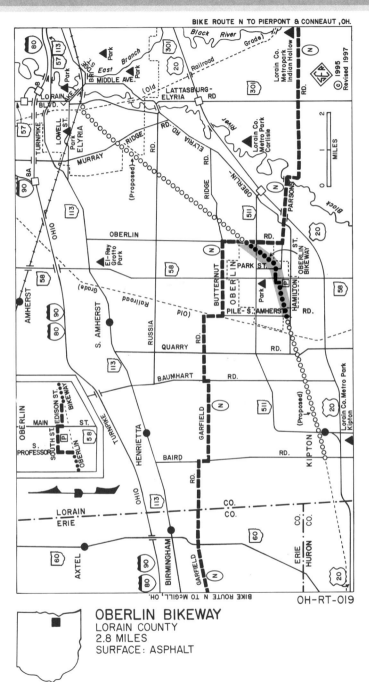

OBERLIN BIKEWAY
LORAIN COUNTY
2.8 MILES
SURFACE: ASPHALT

SLIPPERY ELM TRAIL

VICINITY: *Bowling Green*
TRAIL LENGTH: *12 miles*
SURFACE: *asphalt with paralleling dirt*
TRAIL USE:

The Slippery Elm Trail takes its name from the trees used to build a railroad from Tontogany to Bowling Green in 1874. The original train rails were constructed by applying a thin steel plate on top of elmwood rails. The railroad was extended another 12 miles south to North Baltimore in 1890 and transported coal, freight, lumber, and passengers until the 1960s. It was abandoned in 1978.

Today, a twelve-foot wide asphalt trail with a paralleling bridal path runs from North Baltimore through Rudolph to Bowling Green. Users enjoy relatively flat terrain along the trail's 12 miles. While part of the path passes through the last remainder of the Great Black Swamp, most of its scenery consists of farmland, green meadows, and wooded areas. Trail users can find restaurants in both North Baltimore and Bowling Green.

Long-range plans could link the Slippery Elm Trail to the Miami & Erie Canal Towpath Trail (page 42), the Wabash Cannonball Trail (page 40), and the proposed North Inland Coast Trail to provide Northwest Ohio with a major network of greenways.

PARKING:
Parking for the Slippery Elm Trail can be found directly at each end of the trail in both North Baltimore and Bowling Green.

FOR MORE INFORMATION:
Wood County Park District
18729 Mercer Rd. • Bowling Green, OH 43402
419-353-1897

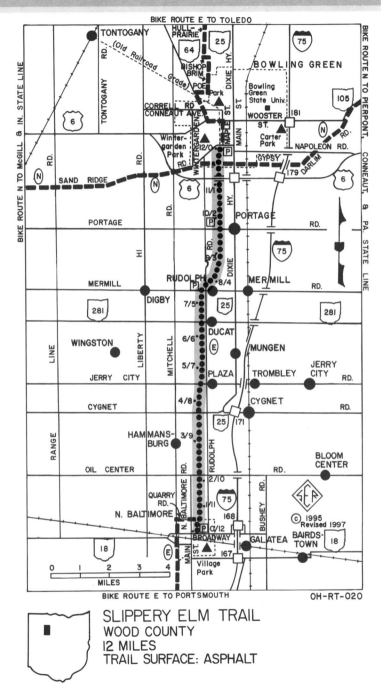

SLIPPERY ELM TRAIL
WOOD COUNTY
12 MILES
TRAIL SURFACE: ASPHALT

49

RICHLAND B. & O. TRAIL
VICINITY: *Richland County*
TRAIL LENGTH: *18.3 miles*
SURFACE: *asphalt*
TRAIL USE:

The Richland B. & O. Trail runs from Butler to Mansfield to form a crescent in the Southern part of Richland County. This rail-trail follows the former Baltimore & Ohio Railroad through the towns of Butler, Bellville, Lexington, and Mansfield, and its scenery includes picturesque farmlands and rolling hills.

The trail begins in Butler, home of the Clear Fork Ski Area and just four miles southwest of Malabar Farm State Park, famous for its homemade maple syrup. The path follows the Clear Fork Mohican River from Butler to Lexington, passing through Bellville and crossing the river five times. In Lexington, where the trail leaves the banks of the Clear Fork Mohican, users can stop to visit the Gorman Nature Center Park and Richland County Historical Society. The trail goes north from Lexington to enter Mansfield from its west side before ending next to North Lake Park. A pedestrian foot bridge guides trail users between the bike path and the park (the bridge's steps may prevent wheelchair use). For further information on the Richland B. & O. Trail, contact the address below.

PARKING:
Parking for this trail can be found in Butler, Bellville, Lexington, Alta, and in North Lake Park on Rowland Street in Mansfield.

FOR MORE INFORMATION:
Gorman Nature Center
2295 Lexington Ave. • *Mansfield, OH 44907*
419-884-3764

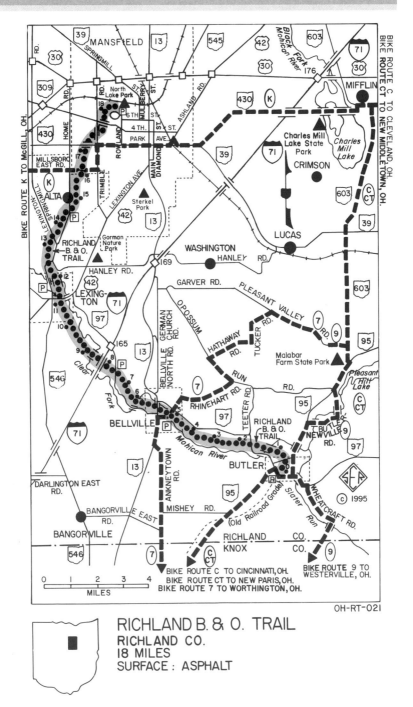

OH-RT-021

RICHLAND B. & O. TRAIL
RICHLAND CO.
18 MILES
SURFACE : ASPHALT

OHIO'S MAJOR BIKE TRAILS

RIVER CORRIDOR BIKEWAY

VICINITY: *Dayton (Great Miami River)*
TRAIL LENGTH: *25 miles*
SURFACE: *asphalt*
TRAIL USE:

The River Corridor Bikeway follows the Great Miami River and the Stillwater River, creating an excellent cycling alternative for Dayton-area commuters. The trail also provides trail users with a relaxing path to walk or bicycle with family and friends without the worry of city traffic. The bikeway traverses much of Montgomery County from south to north as it passes through Miamisburg, West Carrollton, Moraine, and Dayton.

Beginning at the Montogomery-Warren county line off of Cincinnati Pike, the trail follows the Great Miami River Levee through Miamisburg, then parallels Dayton-Cincinnati Pike on its way to West Carrollton; an expanse of grass and trees keeps the bikeway and its users safely separated from the pike. The trail goes around the northwest side of West Carrolton. Traces of the old Miami-Erie Canal can be seen. It then goes to Marina Drive and out of West Carrollton. A 2-mile segment of this section, with no roads in sight, abounds with scenery and serenity. Due to the lack of space for both a road and a

The River Corridor Bikeway crosses a steel span bridge through Island Park.

54

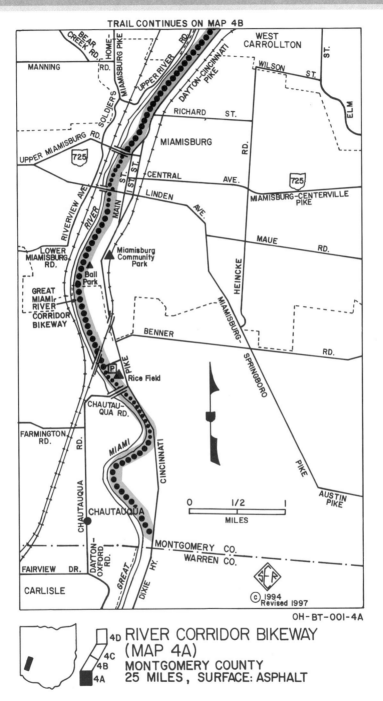

TRAIL CONTINUES ON MAP 4B

WEST CARROLLTON

MANNING

MIAMISBURG

RICHARD ST.

UPPER MIAMISBURG RD.
725

CENTRAL AVE.

LINDEN AVE.

MIAMISBURG-CENTERVILLE PIKE

725

MAUE RD.

LOWER MIAMISBURG RD.

Miamisburg Community Park

Ball Park

GREAT MIAMI RIVER CORRIDOR BIKEWAY

BENNER

RD.

Rice Field

CHAUTAU-QUA RD.

FARMINGTON RD.

MIAMI

CINCINNATI

0   1/2   1
MILES

CHAUTAUQUA

AUSTIN PIKE

MONTGOMERY CO.
WARREN CO.

FAIRVIEW DR.

CARLISLE

© 1994
Revised 1997

OH-BT-OOI-4A

4D **RIVER CORRIDOR BIKEWAY**
4C **(MAP 4A)**
4B MONTGOMERY COUNTY
4A 25 MILES, SURFACE: ASPHALT

bikeway, trail users must use the River Road for about one-half mile before the bikeway resumes to follow the Great Miami River around a bend to the town of Moraine and Old River Park on the south edge of Dayton.

One mile up the trail from Old River Park, trail users encounter the Stewart Avenue Bridge, where the bikeway splits to run up both the east and west side of the river. While both sides of the trail offer a clear view of the bikeway on the opposite side, users that plan to connect with the Wolf Creek Bikeway (page 34) should take the west side. Limited access to both sides of the trail is available between Stewart Avenue and Helena Street, and bicyclists will have to carry their transports up or down stairs; wheelchair users may want to avoid trying to enter or exit the trail at this point. The two trails join together at Helena Street and go north through Island Park where a span bridge takes users across the Stillwater River. The trail then follows the Stillwater River through Triangle and DeWeese Parks in Dayton's north end. The trail ends at Shoup Mill Road.

Future plans for the River Corridor Bikeway include extending it in several directions. The bikeway will eventually follow the Great Miami River south through Warren, Butler, and Hamilton Counties. A new trail, the Mad River Bikeway, will connect the trail to both the Huffman Prairie Overlook Trail (page 28) to Fairborn and the H-Connector Trail to Xenia. Long-range plans will stretch the trail northward to Troy and Piqua. For current information, contact the address below.

PARKING:
Parking for this trail is available at Rice Field next to Cincinnati Pike just south of Miamisburg, along the streets of West Carrollton, at Carillon Park in Moraine along Carillon Boulevard, at Island Park in Dayton along Helena Street, and at Deweese Park in North Dayton along Siben-Thaler Avenue.

FOR MORE INFORMATION:
Miami Valley Regional Bicycle Council, Inc.
400 Miami Valley Tower, 40 W. 4th. St
Dayton, OH 45402 • 513-223-6323

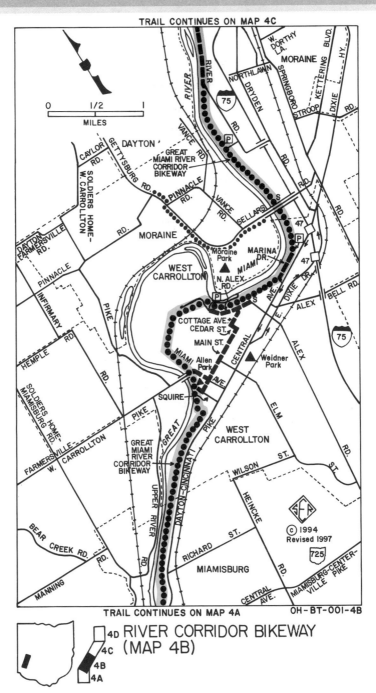

TRAIL CONTINUES ON MAP 4C

RIVER CORRIDOR BIKEWAY (MAP 4B)

OH-BT-001-4B

TRAIL CONTINUES ON MAP 4A

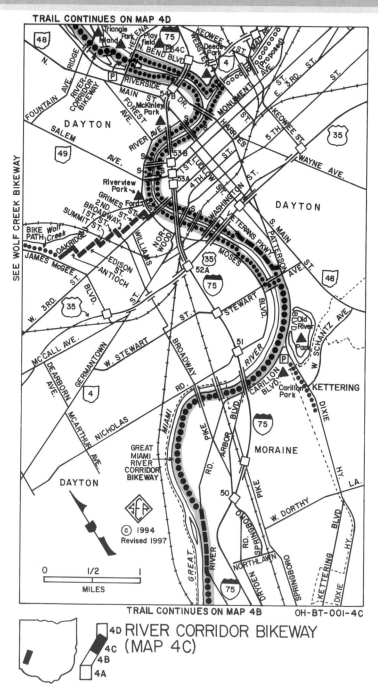

TRAIL CONTINUES ON MAP 4D

TRAIL CONTINUES ON MAP 4B   OH-BT-OOI-4C

□4D RIVER CORRIDOR BIKEWAY
4C (MAP 4C)
4B
4A

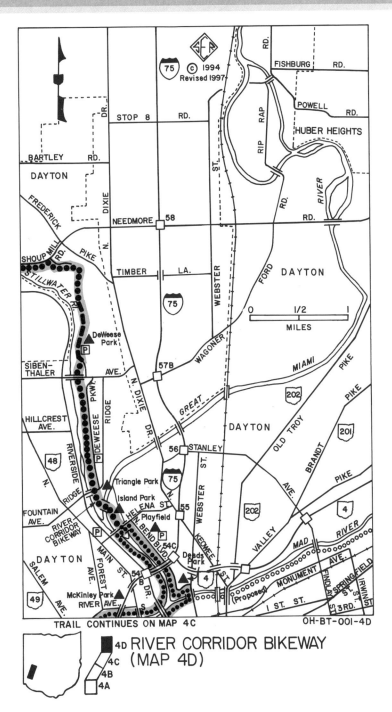

TRAIL CONTINUES ON MAP 4C

OH-BT-OOI-4D

4D RIVER CORRIDOR BIKEWAY
(MAP 4D)
4C
4B
4A

EMERALD NECKLACE TRAIL

VICINITY: *Cleveland*

TRAIL LENGTH: *69 miles (sections incomplete)*

SURFACE: *asphalt*

TRAIL USE:

ASPHALT SECTIONS COMPLETE FROM WEST TO EAST:

Location	Landmarks	Length
Lakewood-Middleburg Heights	Detroit Ave. to Bagley Rd.	13.5 m
Middleburg Heights-Strongsville	Bagley Rd. to W. 130th. St.	8.0 m
Parma-Strongsville	Brookpark Rd.(S.R. 17) to Rocky River Pkwy.	7.5 m
Brecksville Section	Brecksville Rd.(S.R. 21) to Towpath Trail	4.0 m
Walton Hills to Bedford	Alexander Rd (Bike & Hike) to Broadway (S.R. 14)	4.5 m
Bedford-Solon	Broadway (S.R. 14) to New Harper Rd.	6.0 m
Solon-Bentleyville	New Harper Rd. to Miles Rd.	3.5 m
Mayfield-Willoughby Hills	North Chagrin Reservation to Chardon Rd. (U.S. 6)	4.0 m

The Emerald Necklace Trail winds through the Cleveland Metro Parks, a series of reservations created by enthused Clevelanders in 1917 to preserve natural land for future generations. Today the Metro Parks system consists of about 19,000 acres of land on twelve reservations. This beautiful park system provides Cleveland-area residents with outdoor recreation, scenic nature preserves, picnic areas, sporting fields, wildlife management areas, and waterfowl sanctuaries. The system offers biking, hiking, horseback riding, physical fitness trails, golf courses, swimming, boating, and fishing as well as sledding, skating, and cross-country skiing during winter months. Five nature centers in the park system provide nature exhibits and other programs.

At this time, the Emerald Necklace Trail consists of eight separate stretches of paved bicycle paths and utilizes the Cross State Bike Route N to connect several of its sections through the south and southeast end of Cleveland. The six maps on the following pages show both the existing bike paths and the best suitable park roads to take trail users from one trail to another. A bridle path also parallels most of the paved bike paths; but equestrian enthusiasts should contact Cleveland Metro Parks System (address on page 62) for detailed information.

The west side of the Emerald Necklace Trail, along with the Interstate-480 Bikeway (see map on page 63), offers users the best developed

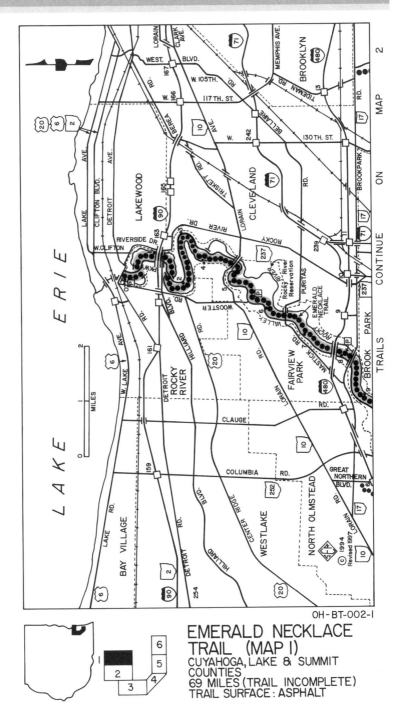

OH-BT-002-1

EMERALD NECKLACE TRAIL (MAP 1)
CUYAHOGA, LAKE & SUMMIT
COUNTIES
69 MILES (TRAIL INCOMPLETE)
TRAIL SURFACE: ASPHALT

61

network of paths. Several paved bike trails totaling 29 miles guide users through the Rocky River Reservation as well as in and out of Lakewood, Rocky River, Fairview Park, Brook Park, North Olmstead, Berea, Parma, Parma Heights, Middleburg Heights, and Strongsville. This network of individual paths starts in Lakewood near Lake Erie on Cleveland's west side and goes south to Strongsville before turning southeast to West 130th Street where the western section ends.

From West 130th Street, trail users join the light traffic of spectacular Valley Parkway to Brecksville Road to access the south side of the Emerald Necklace Trail and four miles of the path's most scenic stretch. This section of trail intersects with the Towpath Trail (page 68) in the Cuyahoga Valley National Recreation Area. To reach the Bedford Reservation, trail users take the Towpath Trail north to Tinkers Creek Road and follow the "Bike Route N" signs to Dunham Road and Gorge Parkway. The parkway takes trail users through the Bedford Reservation where it joins a breathtaking 4.5 mile segment of the Emerald Necklace Trail that negotiates curves and hills and provides a good workout. This same section of path leads south to Alexander Road where it connects to the Bike and Hike Trail (page 6) to Kent.

Two sections of paved bike paths make up the southeastern and eastern portions of the Emerald Necklace Trail. From the Bedford Reservation in Walton Hills, the trail continues 9.5 miles northeast to the South Chagrin Reservation in Bentlyville while a 4-mile network of paved trail runs near Mayfield and Willoughby in the North Chagrin Reservation. Trail users taking the Chagrin River Road between the South and North Chagrin Reservations should use caution:traffic on the road is often quite heavy.

Various extensions and connections are planned for the Emerald Necklace Trail; for current information, write to the address below.

PARKING:
Many parking areas are available all along the Emerald Necklace Trail.

FOR MORE INFORMATION:
Cleveland Metro Parks System
4101 Fulton Pkwy. • Cleveland, OH 44144
216-351-6300

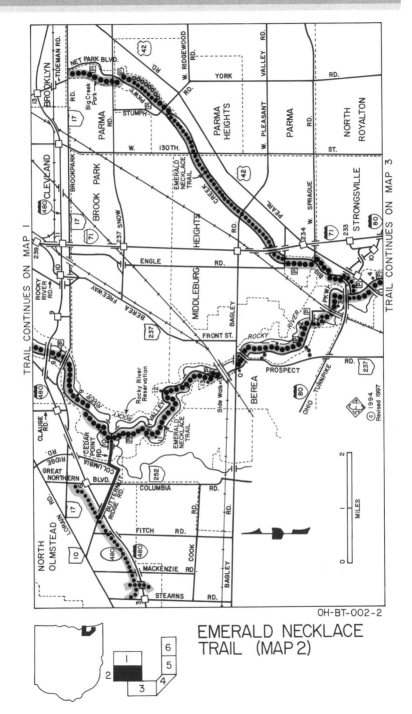

OH-BT-002-2

EMERALD NECKLACE
TRAIL (MAP 2)

MAP 3 • EMERALD NECKLACE TRAIL

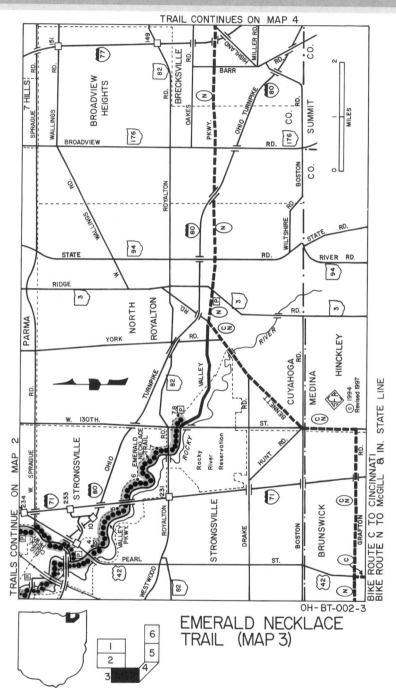

TRAIL CONTINUES ON MAP 4

EMERALD NECKLACE
TRAIL (MAP 3)

OH-BT-002-3

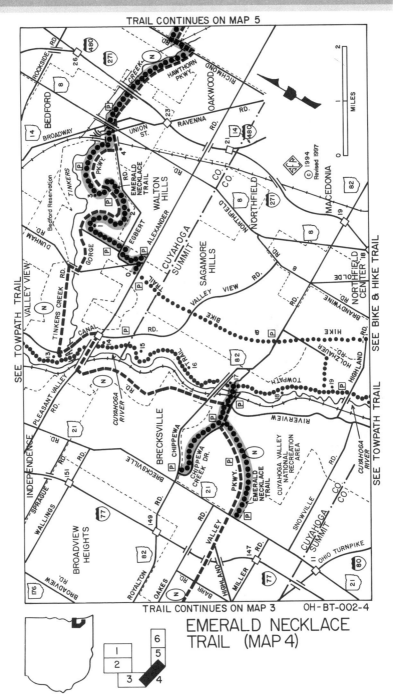

TRAIL CONTINUES ON MAP 5

TRAIL CONTINUES ON MAP 3   OH-BT-002-4

EMERALD NECKLACE
TRAIL (MAP 4)

MAP 5 • EMERALD NECKLACE TRAIL

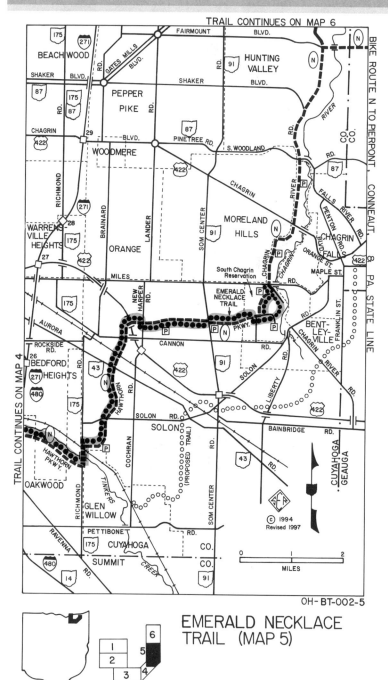

TRAIL CONTINUES ON MAP 6

EMERALD NECKLACE TRAIL (MAP 5)

OH-BT-002-5

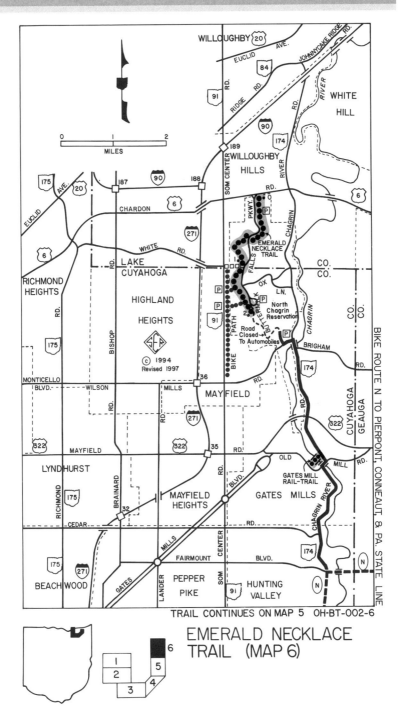

EMERALD NECKLACE
TRAIL (MAP 6)

TRAIL CONTINUES ON MAP 5   OH-BT-002-6

67

TOWPATH TRAIL

VICINITY: *Cleveland/Akron*
TRAIL LENGTH: *19.5 miles*
SURFACE: *smooth crushed gravel*
TRAIL USE:

The Towpath Trail follows the Ohio and Erie Canal along the former canal towpath. At one time the canal ran 309 miles from the Ohio River in Portsmouth to Lake Erie in Cleveland, and mule-pulled barges traveled it for almost ninety years, from 1825 to 1913. The mile markers are based on those once used by canal travelers. These markers, including marker 0 at Lake Erie in Downtown Cleveland, serve as a reminder of the canal and provide Towpath Trail users with a unique way to gauge the distance they've travelled. At mile marker 12, the Canal Visitor Center offers visitors historic information and includes a museum, making it a great place to stop and visit along the trail.

This smooth surfaced trail starts in Cuyahoga County on Rockside Road at mile marker 11 and runs all the way into Summit County on Bath Road at mile marker 30, taking users from Cleveland to Akron and passing through the center of the Cuyahoga Valley National Recreation Area as it parallels the Cuyahoga River.

From Rockside Road to State Route 82 at mile marker 17, water still runs through the canal and trail users can enjoy seeing old locks. Near this same mile marker, the Towpath Trail intersects with the Emerald Necklace Trail (page 60) as it runs west to Brecksville through the Brecksville Reservation. South from this same intersection, the old canal beds lie empty or have become wetlands and home to an abundance of wildlife. Near mile marker 19 the trail intersects the Old Carriage Trail, which leads up a long hill to connect with the 29-mile Bike & Hike Trail (page 6) to both Bedford or to Kent.

Continuing south, the Towpath Trail takes users into Boston near mile marker 21 where there is a youth hostel. Between Boston and Peninsula, the trail becomes a long wood-decked "bridge" to traverse a large wetland. The trail also passes under the Interstate 271 and Interstate 80 (Ohio Turnpike) bridges on its way to the antique shops, stores, and restaurant of historic Peninsula at mile marker 24. Active

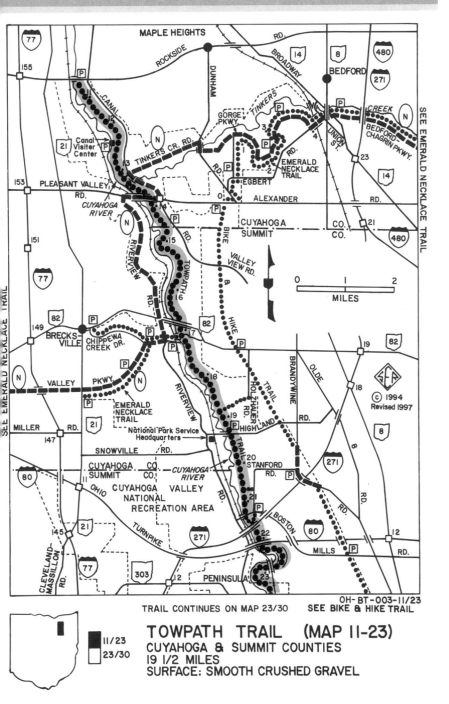

TRAIL CONTINUES ON MAP 23/30   SEE BIKE & HIKE TRAIL

OH-BT-003-11/23

TOWPATH TRAIL (MAP 11-23)
CUYAHOGA & SUMMIT COUNTIES
19 1/2 MILES
SURFACE: SMOOTH CRUSHED GRAVEL

11/23
23/30

passenger excursion trains also pass through Peninsula (for more information on the train excursions, write to the address on page 70).

From Peninsula, the trail heads south over another expanse of wetland on a wooden-decked bridge to Ira Road and the Hale Farm and Village at mile marker 28. Unfortunately, a stretch of the old canal bed between Ira Road and Bath Road was destroyed while constructing Riverview Road, and only remnants of a few locks remain along this stretch of the Towpath Trail. The trail ends at mile marker 30 in Akron's north end.

Future plans involve extending the trail in both directions. It will eventually stretch north to Downtown Cleveland at Lake Erie's mile marker 0. Akron plans to extend the Towpath Trail through the city and beyond, and the Towpath Trail may eventually become part of the Ohio-to-Erie Trail creating a trail that could take users from Cleveland to Columbus to Cincinnati.

PARKING:
Parking is available at the Canal Visitor Center (mile marker 12) and at the trail's end in Akron (mile marker 30).

FOR MORE INFORMATION:	
Cuyahoga Valley National Recreation Area 15610 Vaughn Rd. Brecksville, OH 44141	Ohio-Erie Canal Corridor Coalition 520 S. Main • Akron, OH 44311 330-434-5657

The Towpath Trail follows the old Ohio-Erie Canal (near mile marker 12).

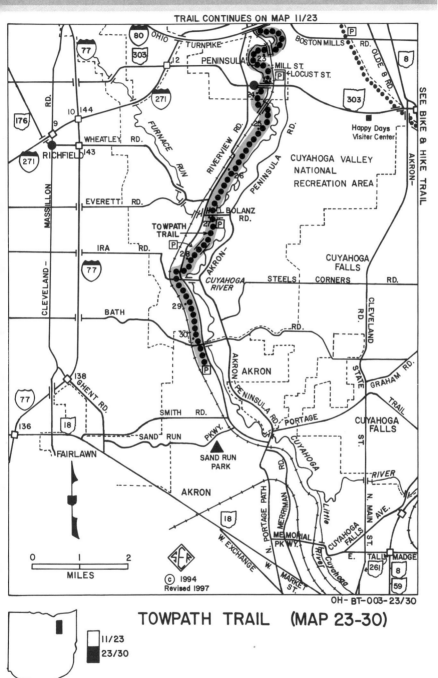

TOWPATH TRAIL (MAP 23-30)

OH- BT-003-23/30

71

OHIO'S
MINOR &
POTENTIAL
RAIL-TRAILS

OHIO'S MINOR RAIL-TRAILS

CALIFORNIA JUNCTION TRAIL
VICINITY: Hamilton County, in California Ohio. *Trail runs through the California Woods Nature Preserve near U.S. 52.*

TRAIL LENGTH: 1 mile

SURFACE: *original ballast & wood chips*

TRAIL USE:

FOR MORE INFORMATION: *California Woods Outdoor Recreation Center*
5400 Kellogg Avenue
Cincinnati, OH 45228
513-231-8678

MARBLEHEAD TRAIL
VICINITY: Ottawa County. *Trail follows S.R. 163 from Lakeside to Marblehead.*

TRAIL LENGTH: 2 miles

SURFACE: *original ballast*

TRAIL USE:

FOR MORE INFORMATION: *Address & phone number unavailable.*

HURON TRAIL
VICINITY: Erie County, *follows U.S. 6 in Huron from the high school to the elementary school.*

TRAIL LENGTH: 1.5 miles

SURFACE: *original ballast*

TRAIL USE:

FOR MORE INFORMATION: *City of Huron, Division of Streets & Parks*
608 Rye Beach Road
Huron, OH 44839
419-433-5000

GATES MILLS TRAIL

VICINITY: Cuyahoga County. Trail follows Old Mill Road over Chagrin River in Gates Mills from Old Mill Road to Chagrin River Road. See Emerald Necklace Trail, Map 6, on page 67.

TRAIL LENGTH: .25 mile

SURFACE: asphalt

TRAIL USE:

FOR MORE INFORMATION: Address & phone number unavailable.

DARKE COUNTY PARK DISTRICT TRAIL

VICINITY: Darke County, Greenville. Trail crosses over Greenville Creek between East Water Street and North Broadway.

TRAIL LENGTH: .5 mile

SURFACE: concrete and asphalt

TRAIL USE:

FOR MORE INFORMATION: Darke County Park District
603 South Broadway
Greenville, OH 45331-1929
513-548-0165

A 1940's-era passenger train—a predecessor to many of the bike trails that exist today.

OHIO'S POTENTIAL RAIL-TRAILS

PROPOSED TRAIL NAME	MILES	END POINTS OF TRAIL
A. C. & Y. Trail	27	Delphos to Bluffton
Athens to Belpre Trail	34	Athens to Belpre
Athens to Nelsonville Bikeway	13	Athens to Nelsonville
Athens to Zaleski	18	Athens to Zaleski
Cincinnati Riverfront Trail	11	Cincinnati; Downtown Area to Lunken Airport
Clinton Rail-Trail	30	Morrow to Sabina
Elyria to Oberlin to Kipton Trail	12	Elyria to Kipton
Gallia County Bikeway	26	Kanauga to Gallipolis to Minerton
H-Connector Trail	20	Dayton to Xenia
Headwaters Trail	7	Mantua to Garretsville
Holmes County Trail	34	Brinkhave to Fredericksburg
Huron River Greenway	6	Huron to Milan
Lake County Greenway	7	Painesville; Fairport Harbor to Lake-Geauga County Line
Maple Highlands Trail	14	Chardon to Bundysburg
Massillon to Dalton Trail	6	Massillon to Dalton
Nelsonville to Shawnee Bikeway	19	Nelsonville to Shawnee
North Inland Coast Trail	49	Millbury to Norwalk
Ohio to Erie Trail	320	Cincinnati to Columbus to Cleveland
Perry County Trail	31	Thornville to Shawnee
SWOTA Trail	7	Valley Junction to Harrison (Ohio-Indiana State Line)
Towners Woods Rail-Trail	29	Kent - Warren
Tri-County Triangle Trail	59	Chillicothe to Washington C.H. & Hillsboro
Western Reserve Greenway	75	Ashtabula to East Liverpool
Westerville Bikeway	3	Westerville; Schrock Road to Maxtown Road
Xenia-Jamestown Bikeway	10	Xenia-Jamestown

For more information on receiving the developments of each trail, contact the Ohio Chapter of the Rails-to-Trails Conservancy, 692 N. High Street., Suite 211, Columbus, OH 43215 or call 614-224-8707.

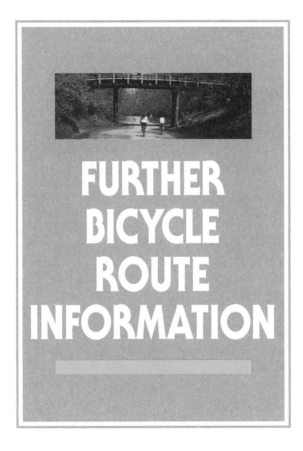

FURTHER
BICYCLE
ROUTE
INFORMATION

COLUMBUS OUTDOOR PURSUITS BIKE ROUTE MAPS

(FORMERLY COLUMBUS COUNCIL OF AYH)

The bike maps listed below have been produced by the Columbus Outdoor Pursuits, a recreational club in Central Ohio. To order maps, photocopy this page, complete the form, enclose a check for the appropriate amount made out to the Columbus Outdoor Pursuits, and mail it to: Columbus Outdoor Pursuits, P.O. Box 14384, Columbus, OH, 43214 (614-447-1006). Make sure to include your name, address, and telephone number.

ROUTE	LENGTH	DESCRIPTION	PRICE	#
Bike Route A	247 m.	Elizabeth Town-Toledo	$5.00	___
Bike Route B	240 m.	Cincinnati -Marietta	$5.00	___
Bike Route C	283 m.	Cincinnati-Cleveland	$5.00	___
Cardinal Trail	313 m.	New Paris-Petersburg	$5.00	___
Bike Route E	253 m.	Portsmouth-Toledo	$5.00	___
Bike Route F	301 m.	New Paris-Dilles Bottom	$5.00	___
Bike Route J	246 m.	Marietta-Conneaut	$5.00	___
Bike Route K	164 m.	Payne-Mifflin	$5.00	___
Bike Route N	311 m.	McGill-Pierpont & Conneaut.		
Bike Route 1	10 m.	Xenia-Yellow Springs (see the Little Miami Scenic Trail, Map 3, p. 17 in this book)		
Bike Route 2	4 m.	Upper Arlington-Columbus (See Columbus Ohio & Franklin County Bike Route Guide, below)		
Bike Route 5	75 m.	Caesar Creek State Park-Columbus. FREE		___
Bike Route 7	64 m.	Worthington-Malabar Farm State Park		
Bike Route 9	61 m.	Westerville-Malabar Farm State Park		

OTHER MAPS BY THE COLUMBUS OUTDOOR PURSUITS

36 New Bike Routes in Mid-Ohio (Book of Loop Route Maps)	$5.00	___
Columbus Ohio & Franklin County Bicycle Route Guide (Folding Multicolor Map)	$5.00	___
Total Cost of Maps Ordered (amount enclosed)	$	___

COLUMBUS OUTDOOR PURSUITS
BIKE ROUTE MAPS

OHIO PUBLISHED BICYCLE MAPS

OHIO (STATEWIDE COVERAGE)

Ohio Bicycle Route Guide. Ohio Department of Transportation, Bicycle Transportation, 25 S. Front St., Columbus, OH 43216.

614-466-4930   A set of 19 maps. Scale: 1 in. = 3 miles.

A. FRANKLIN COUNTY (COLUMBUS)

Columbus Ohio & Franklin County Bicycle Route Guide, Columbus Council of American Youth Hostels, P.O. Box 14384, Columbus, OH 43214.

614-447-1006   Scale: 1 in. = 1.5 miles.

B. HAMILTON COUNTY (CINCINNATI)

OKI Bike Route Guides for Butler, Clermont, Hamilton, and Warren Counties., OKI-Regional Council of Governments, 801-B, W. 8th St., Suite 400, Cincinnati, OH 45203.

513-621-7060   Set of 4 maps. Scale: 1 in. = 2 miles.

C. HANCOCK COUNTY (FINDLAY)

Findlay and Hancock County Bike Route System, Hancock Park District, 819 Park St., 1833 Courthouse, Findlay, OH 45480.

419-423-6952   Scale: 1 in. = 1.5 miles.

D. LICKING COUNTY (NEWARK)

"*Licking County Bicycle & Pedestrian Transportation Corridor Map,*" Thomas J. Evans Foundation, 36 N. 2nd St., P.O. Box 919, Newark, OH 43058-0919.

614-349-3863   Scale: 1 in. = 4 miles

E. MONTGOMERY COUNTY (DAYTON)

Metro Dayton by Bicycle, Miami Valley Regional Bicycle Council, Inc., 400 Miami Valley Tower, 40 W. 4th St., Dayton, OH 45402.

513-223-6323   A set of 8 maps. Scale: 2.6 in. = 1 miles

F. IOWA TO MAINE ROUTE

Adventure Cycling Association, P.O. Box 8308, Missoula, MT. 59807-8308.

800-721-8719.   Scale: 1 in. = 4 mi.

PUBLISHED BICYCLE MAPS IN OHIO

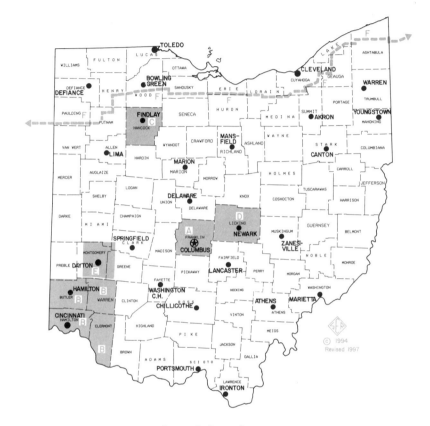

Youth Hostels (U.S.A.)

American Youth Hostels
733 15th. St. NW, Suite 480
Washington, DC 20005
202-783-6161

Additional Youth Hostels
The Hostel Handbook
722 St. Nicholas Ave.
New York, NY 10031
212-926-7030

ote: For current prices, contact the appropriate offices. Readers can obtain a
ee Ohio highway map by writing to the Ohio Department of
ransportation Bicycle Transportation, 25 South Front Street, Room 118,
olumbus, OH 43216.

U.S. RAILS-TO-TRAILS GUIDEBOOKS

U.S. GENERAL

700 Great Rail-Trails: A National Directory of Multi-Use Paths Created from Abandoned Railroads. Rails-to-Trails Conservancy, 1995, 1100 17th. St. NW, 10th Floor, Washington, DC 20036.

A listing of trails for all 50 States. Maps not included.

CALIFORNIA

Rail-Trail Guide To California, 1995, Infinty Press, P.O. Box 17883, Seattle, WA 98107

Maps Included.

ILLINOIS

Illinois Rail-Trails, Rails-to-Trails Conservancy, 1992, RTC, 1100 17th. St. NW, 10th Floor, Washington, DC 20036.

Maps Included.

Bicycle Trails of Illinois, 1996, American Bike Trails, 1257 S. Milwaukee Ave., Libertyville, IL 60048.

Maps Included.

IOWA

Bicycle Trails of Iowa, 1996, American Bike Trails, 1257 S. Milwaukee Ave., Libertyville, IL 60048.

Maps Included.

MINNESOTA

Biking Minnesota's Rail-Trails, Marlys Mickelson, 1997, Adventure Publications, Inc., P.O. Box 269, Cambridge, MN 55008.

Maps Included; book also shows some trails in Wisconsin.

NEW ENGLAND STATES (CT, MA, ME, NH, RI, VT)

Great Rail-Trails of the Northeast, 1995, New England Cartographics, Inc. P.O. Box 9369, North Amherst, MA 01059

OHIO

Biking Ohio's Rail-Trails, Shawn E. Richardson, 1997,
Adventure Publications, Inc., P.O. Box 269, Cambridge, MN
55008.
Maps Included.

PENNSYLVANIA

Pennsylvania's Great Rail-Trails, Rails-to-Trails Conservancy, 1994, RTC,
1100 17th. St. NW, 10th Floor, Washington, DC 20036.
Maps Included.

WASHINGTON STATE

Washington's Rail-Trails, Fred Wert, 1992, The Mountaineers, 1011 SW
Klickitat Way, Seattle, WA 98134.
Maps Included.

WEST VIRGINIA

Adventure Guide to WV Rail-Trails, 1995, West Virginia Rails-to-Trails
Council, P.O. Box 8889, South Charleston, WV 25303-0889.
Maps included.

WISCONSIN

Biking Wisconsin's Rail-Trails, Shawn E. Richardson, 1997, Adventure
Publications, Inc., P.O. Box 269, Cambridge, MN 55008.
Maps Included.

OHIO TRAILS INDEX AND ADDRESSES

RAILS TO TRAILS CONSERVANCY MEMBERSHIP

To join the Rail-to-Trails Conservancy or give a gift membership to someone else, simply photocopy and complete this form and mail it along with the appropriate membership fee to the address below.

Name _____

Street _____

City, State, Zip _____

Phone (include area code): (h) _____ (w) _____

Membership level (check the appropriate box):

Individual Membership $18.00   ☐
Family Membership $25.00   ☐
Sustaining Membership $35.00   ☐
Patron Membership $50.00   ☐
Benefactor Membership $100.00   ☐

Enclose a check payable to Rails-to-Trails Conservancy and mail this form to:

Rails-to-Trails Conservancy
Shipping Department
P.O. Box 295
Federalsburg, MD 21632-0295

To join by using your Mastercard or Visa, call 800-888-7747.

BICYCLE
SAFETY AND
EQUIPMENT

BICYCLE SAFETY

Fortunately, accidents and injury are not common in bicycling, especially beyond the exuberance of youth. But they do happen and certainly detract from the enjoyment of a bike trip.

Common sense and awareness are the best policy. Even the most experienced among us can benefit from a periodic refresher course on the subject, so store the following safety tips in your memory bank:

GENERAL BICYCLING SAFETY TIPS

1. *Obey traffic laws* and *obey traffic signs.* Most serious accidents involve motor vehicles and drivers are conditioned to expect you to do as another motor vehicle would.

2. Go with the traffic flow, signal your turns and lane changes and be especially alert for pedestrians or car doors opening when passing a line of parked cars or other roadside obstructions. Stay as close to the right side of the road as possible.

3. Yield the right-of-way to vehicles or pedestrians. Be prepared to do so even if you have the right-of-way. A bicycle is hardly the vehicle for practicing that a good offense is the best defense.

4. Wear an approved helmet. This is one of the most important precautions you can take to avoid serious injury. (See Mayo Clinic article on the subject, page 93.)

5. Plan your ride so you are off the streets, roads and trails by dusk. Bicycles are best left parked or stored at night, but if you must, be sure you have front, side and rear reflectors, plus lights. Wear or switch to light–colored clothing.

6. Give an audible signal before passing pedestrians or other cyclists. We recommend a bike bell. Many bicyclists call out "Passing on your left!" to warn their fellow trail users of their approach.

RAIL-TRAIL COURTESY & COMMON SENSE

1. Stay on designated trails.

2. Bicyclists use the right side of the trail (walkers use the left side of the trail).

3. Bicyclists should only pass slower users on the left side of the trail; use your voice to warn others when you need to pass (see #6, above).

4. Get off to the side of the trail if you need to stop.

5. Bicyclists should yield to all other users.

6. Use a light at night.

7. Do not use alcohol and drugs while on the trail.

8. Do not litter.

9. Do not trespass onto adjacent land.

10. Do not wear headphones while using the trail.

Several steel trestles from the old railroads are still in tact like this one on the Kokosing Gap Trail (see page 24).

AWARENESS:

1. Give your bike a pre-ride check. This is not only for maintenance. Good brakes and a mechanically sound bike are necessary for maximum safety and enjoyment. Check your tire pressure every week. Keep your tires inflated to the pressure noted on the side of the tire.

2. When planning a trip, be aware of your own capabilities as well as the limitations and health of your friends. A ride which tests one's outer limits is best left to those conditioned to do so.

3. Be alert to changing conditions. Rain will muffle the sound of approaching vehicles and generate slippery conditions, especially after a long period without rain. (Roadway oil and grime can be hazardous until the rain washes them away.)

4. Watch for road debris or loose rocks or gravel. Slow down if these is excessive debris or broken road surface. Learn to guide your bike very straight and vertical through loose sand or rocks. If you find a short stretch of loose sand it would even pay to practice riding through it a few times to give you needed confidence when it surprises you along the trail.

5. The old Irish prayer "May the wind blow always at your back" is only partially true for bicyclists. Be prepared for the vacuum effect of passing vehicles, sudden gusts of sudden absences when passing roadside buildings, trees or other shelter.

6. A word about dogs, many of whom seem to take particular objection to bicycles. If you encounter one, the first requirement is not to panic. If the dog is only testing, and not actually attacking, a shout or order may keep it at bay. If it is very aggressive, the best defense is to dismount, keeping the bike between you and the dog. Grab anything available to throw or pretend to throw. Most of all, keep moving as a dog is only going to defend what it perceives to be the limits of its territory.

BICYCLE HEADGEAR

Protective headgear can be a lifesaver. With an increasing number of people riding bicycles on our streets and highways, the risk of injury —in particular, head injury—continues to rise. Each year, nearly 50,000 bicyclists suffer serious head injuries. According to the most recent statistics, head injuries are the leading cause of death in the approximately 1,300 bicycle-related fatalities that occur annually. To a large extent, these head injuries are preventable.

WEARING A HELMET CAN MAKE A DIFFERENCE

Until recently, advocates of the use of protective headgear for cyclists found their stance lacked scientific support. But wearing protective headgear clearly make a difference. Recent evidence confirms that a helmet can reduce your risk of serious head and brain injury by almost 90 percent should you be involved in a bicycle accident.

Bicycle riding is an excellent form of aerobic exercise that can benefit your musculoskeletal and cardiovascular systems. Make the investment in a helmet and take the time to put it on each time you ride.

continued...

The Skyline of Columbus, Ohio, along the Olentangy-Scioto River Bikeway (see page 2).

WHAT TO LOOK FOR IN A BICYCLE HELMET

We endorse these guidelines for bicycle helmets recommended by the American Academy of Pediatrics:

- The helmet should meet the voluntary testing standards of one of these two groups: American National Standards Institute (ANSI) or Snell Memorial Foundation. Look for a sticker on the inside of helmet.

- Select the right size. Find one that fits comfortably and doesn't pinch.

- Buy a helmet with a durable outer shell and a polystyrene liner. Be sure it allows adequate ventilation.

- Use the adjustable foam pads to ensure a proper fit at the front, back and sides.

- Adjust the strap for a snug fit. The helmet should cover the top of your forehead and not rock side to side or back and forth with the chin strap in place.

- Replace your helmet if it is involved in an accident.

"Bicycle Headgear" reprinted from July 1989 "Mayo Clinic Health Letter" with permission of Mayo Foundation, for Medical Education and Research, Rochester, Minnesota

SPECIAL EQUIPMENT

When venturing out on bicycle tours, it is always smart to take along equipment to help make roadside adjustments and repairs. It is not necessary for every member of your group to carry a complete set of equipment, but make sure someone in your group brings along the equipment listed below:

1. Standard or slotted screwdriver.

2. Phillip's screwdriver

3. 6" or 8" adjustable wrench.

4. Small pliers.

5. Spoke adjuster.

6. Tire pressure gauge.

7. Portable tire pump.

8. Spare innertube.

9. Tire-changing lugs.

While many trails have rest areas, this one along the Nickelplate Trail (see page 32) has been made more safe by leaving old railroad ties in place to serve as speed bumps.

ABOUT THE AUTHOR

Shawn E. Richardson has worked as a cartographer for the Ohio Department of Transportation since 1988. He specializes in photogrammetry, the process of creating maps using aerial photography. He received his Bachelor of Science degree in environmental geography with an emphasis on cartography from Kentucky's University of Louisville in 1985. A Kentucky native, Shawn has lived in Ohio since 1988.

Shawn enjoys bicycle touring, and his excursions can last anywhere from a few hours to several days. Although he has biked back roads through many states, the majority of his touring has been on trails.

He is an active member of the Ohio Rails-to-Trails Conservancy and has belonged to the the Columbus Council of American Youth Hostels and to the Louisville Wheelman.

Biking Ohio's Rail-Trails is Shawn's first book. If you have questions or comments for Shawn, You can contact him by writing : Shawn E. Richardson, Biking USA's Rail-Trails, PO Box 284, Hilliard, OH 43026-0284.

Author Shawn E. Richardson